Amel Selmi

Grundwissen Englisch inklusiv

Grammatik 6. Klasse Inklusionsmaterial

Die Autorin

Amel Selmi ist seit Jahren im Gemeinsamen Lernen aktiv. Seit 2011 unterrichtet sie Kinder mit und ohne sonderpädagogischen Unterstützungsbedarf in den Fächern Englisch und Sport. Ihre verfassten Titel basieren auf langjährigen Erfahrungen, die sie an unterschiedlichen Schulen und Schulformen sammeln konnte, und ermöglichen die praktische Umsetzung inklusiven Unterrichts – aus der Praxis für die Praxis. Im Rahmen der konzeptionellen Ausrichtung erstellt Amel Selmi Vorschläge und Konzepte, wie Inklusion effektiv und schülerorientiert umgesetzt werden kann.

Gedruckt auf umweltbewusst gefertigtem, chlorfrei gebleichtem und alterungsbeständigem Papier.

1. Auflage 2022
© 2022 Persen Verlag, Hamburg
AAP Lehrerwelt GmbH
Veritaskai 3
21079 Hamburg
Telefon: +49 (0) 40325083-040
E-Mail: info@lehrerwelt.de
Geschäftsführung: Christian Glaser
USt-ID: DE 173 77 61 42
Register: AG Hamburg HRB/126335
Alle Rechte vorbehalten.

Das Werk als Ganzes sowie in seinen Teilen unterliegt dem deutschen Urheberrecht. Der Erwerber einer Einzellizenz des Werkes ist berechtigt, das Werk als Ganzes oder in seinen Teilen für den eigenen Gebrauch und den Einsatz im eigenen Präsenz- wie auch dem Distanzunterricht zu nutzen.
Produkte, die aufgrund ihres Bestimmungszweckes zur Vervielfältigung und Weitergabe zu Unterrichtszwecken gedacht sind (insbesondere Kopiervorlagen und Arbeitsblätter), dürfen zu Unterrichtszwecken vervielfältigt und weitergegeben werden.

Die Nutzung ist nur für den genannten Zweck gestattet, nicht jedoch für einen schulweiten Einsatz und Gebrauch, für die Weiterleitung an Dritte einschließlich weiterer Lehrkräfte, für die Veröffentlichung im Internet oder in (Schul-)Intranets oder einen weiteren kommerziellen Gebrauch.
Mit dem Kauf einer Schullizenz ist die Schule berechtigt, die Inhalte durch alle Lehrkräfte des Kollegiums der erwerbenden Schule sowie durch die Schülerinnen und Schüler der Schule und deren Eltern zu nutzen.

Nicht erlaubt ist die Weiterleitung der Inhalte an Lehrkräfte, Schülerinnen und Schüler, Eltern, andere Personen, soziale Netzwerke, Downloaddienste oder Ähnliches außerhalb der eigenen Schule.
Eine über den genannten Zweck hinausgehende Nutzung bedarf in jedem Fall der vorherigen schriftlichen Zustimmung des Verlags.
Sind Internetadressen in diesem Werk angegeben, wurden diese vom Verlag sorgfältig geprüft. Da wir auf die externen Seiten weder inhaltliche noch gestalterische Einflussmöglichkeiten haben, können wir nicht garantieren, dass die Inhalte zu einem späteren Zeitpunkt noch dieselben sind wie zum Zeitpunkt der Drucklegung. Der PERSEN Verlag übernimmt deshalb keine Gewähr für die Aktualität und den Inhalt dieser Internetseiten oder solcher, die mit ihnen verlinkt sind, und schließt jegliche Haftung aus.

Wir verwenden in unseren Werken eine gendernneutrale Sprache. Wenn keine neutrale Formulierung möglich ist, nennen wir die weibliche und die männliche Form. In Fällen, in denen wir aufgrund einer besseren Lesbarkeit nur ein Geschlecht nennen können, achten wir darauf, den unterschiedlichen Geschlechtsidentitäten gleichermaßen gerecht zu werden.

Autorin:	Amel Selmi
Covergestaltung:	TSA&B Werbeagentur GmbH, Hamburg
Illustrationen:	Stefan Lucas (Covergrafik)
Satz:	Satzpunkt Ursula Ewert GmbH, Bayreuth
Druck und Bindung:	Design and printing JSC KOPA, Litauen

ISBN: 978-3-403-20773-3
www.persen.de

Inhaltsverzeichnis

1. **Vorwort** 5

2. **Methodisch-didaktische Hinweise**
   2.1 Sprache und Kommunikation 5
   2.2 Kompetenzerwartungen 5
   2.3 Inklusion und Lernen 5
   2.4 Zu den Übungen 6
   2.5 Merkmale auf einen Blick 6

1 Kopiervorlagen Revision Grammar

Revision Grammar I – Grammar Box: Simple Present 7
Simple Present: Aussagen 8
Simple Present: Aussagen 10
Simple Present: Verneinung 12
Simple Present: Verneinung 13
Simple Present: Fragen 14
Simple Present: Fragen 15
Revision Grammar II – Grammar Box: Simple Past 16
Simple Past: Aussagen 17
Simple Past: Aussagen 20
Simple Past: Verneinung 24
Simple Past: Verneinung 26
Simple Past: Fragen 28
Simple Past: Fragen 32
Revision Grammar III – Grammar Box: Das Verb *to be* 37
To be: Übungen 38
To be: Übungen 40
Grammar Mix: Simple Past vs. Simple Present .. 42
Grammar Mix: Simple Past vs. Simple Present .. 44
Übersicht: Irregular verbs 46
Übung: Irregular verbs 47
Übung: Irregular verbs 48

2 Adjektive

Grammar Box: Adjectives 49
Adjektive: Steigerung und Vergleich 50
Adjektive: Steigerung und Vergleich 56

3 Adverbien

Grammar Box: Adverbs 63
Adverbien: Übungen 64
Adverbien: Übungen 66

4 Possessivpronomen

Grammar Box: Possessive Pronouns 68
Possessivpronomen: Übungen 69
Possessivpronomen: Übungen 71

5 Mengenangaben

Grammar Box: *some* and *any* / *much* and *many* 73
Mengenangaben: *some* and *any* 74
Mengenangaben: *some* and *any* 76
Mengenangaben: *much* and *many* 78
Mengenangaben: *much* and *many* 80

6 Present Perfect

Grammar Box: Present Perfect 82
Present Perfect: Aussagen 84
Present Perfect: Aussagen 87
Present Perfect: Verneinung 90
Present Perfect: Verneinung 91
Present Perfect: Fragen 92
Present Perfect: Fragen 93

7 Going-to-Future

Grammar Box: Going-to-Future 94
Going-to-Future: Aussagen 95
Going-to-Future: Aussagen 97
Going-to-Future: Verneinung 99
Going-to-Future: Verneinung 100
Going-to-Future: Fragen 101
Going-to-Future: Fragen 102

8 Will-Future

Grammar Box: Will-Future 103
Will-Future: Aussagen 104
Will-Future: Aussagen 105
Will-Future: Verneinung 106
Will-Future: Verneinung 108
Will-Future: Fragen 110
Will-Future: Fragen 111

Inhaltsverzeichnis

9 If-Satz Typ I

Grammar Box: If Clause Type I.............112

If-Satz Typ I: Übungen....................113

If-Satz Typ I: Übungen....................116

Abbildungsverzeichnis.....................**119**

Grau unterlegte Arbeitsblätter im Inhaltsverzeichnis sind die Arbeitsblätter für die Lernenden mit sonderpädagogischem Förderbedarf.

Digitales Zusatzmaterial:
Lösungen zu den Arbeitsblättern

1. Vorwort

Das vorliegende Übungsbuch umfasst die grammatischen Themenfelder, die für den Englischunterricht der 6. Jahrgangsstufe vorgesehen sind. Es eignet sich besonders für einen leistungsdifferenzierten inklusiven Unterricht und ist dabei unabhängig vom Lehrwerk einsetzbar. In verschiedene Themenbereiche untergliedert, beinhaltet das Übungsbuch Kopiervorlagen, die sowohl von lernstarken als auch von lernschwachen Schülerinnen und Schülern bearbeitet werden können. Diese Differenzierung und die Unterteilung in einfache und schwierige Aufgaben bietet zudem die Möglichkeit, allen Lernenden den Lernstoff nachhaltig zu vermitteln und auf diese Weise ein einheitliches Klassenergebnis zu erzielen. Dabei steht vor allem die individuelle Förderung der Lernenden im Vordergrund, die durch eine leistungsheterogene Aufteilung und Differenzierung der Aufgabentypen gewährleistet ist. Ihnen wird auffallen, dass die Übungen für lernschwache Schülerinnen und Schüler weniger abstrakt und überschaubarer gestaltet sind, während lernstarke Schülerinnen und Schüler herausforderndere Aufgaben ausfüllen. Das Übungsbuch eignet sich für die ganze Klasse und bietet durch eine hohe Anzahl an Übungsvarianten eine hervorragende Möglichkeit, grammatikalische Kenntnisse und Sprachgebrauch zu vertiefen. Kopiervorlagen für lernschwache Schülerinnen und Schüler sind zusätzlich mit zweisprachigen Aufgabenanleitungen versehen. Bitte beachten Sie, dass die Erläuterungen der Aufgaben zum besseren Verständnis und zur besseren Lesbarkeit sinngemäß und nicht wortwörtlich übersetzt sind. Dies erleichtert Lernschwächeren die Arbeit erheblich und versetzt sie in die Lage, die Aufgaben selbstständig zu bearbeiten.

2. Methodisch-didaktische Hinweise

2.1 Sprache und Kommunikation

Der Gebrauch einer Sprache setzt einen grundlegenden Wortschatz und die korrekte Nutzung grammatikalischer Regeln voraus. Um sowohl Fallen in der Grammatik als auch im Sprachgebrauch zu vermeiden, ist es wichtig, Basiswissen zu erlernen und in möglichst vielfältigen Anwendungen zu üben. Die Inhalte dieses Buches bieten eine optimale Möglichkeit, die englische Grammatik kleinschrittig und systematisch zu vertiefen und somit z. B. ideal auf Klassenarbeiten vorbereitet zu sein. Abwechslungsreiche und individuelle Übungen für den strukturierten Grammatikerwerb führen zu einem zunehmend sicheren Umgang mit der englischen Sprache und erweitern erheblich die kommunikativen Fähigkeiten.

2.2 Kompetenzerwartungen

Das hier vorliegende Übungsbuch ist auf die Kompetenzerwartungen des Englischunterrichts in der 6. Jahrgangsstufe ausgerichtet. Schritt für Schritt werden die vorgesehenen Themen, Inhalte und entsprechenden Arbeitsaufträge kapitelweise abgedeckt. Zudem bietet dieser Band eine Wiederholung bekannter Zeitformen und eine kurze Erklärung der Grammatik („Grammar Box").

Die Schüler und Schülerinnen lernen …
- die Zeiten anzuwenden
- Adjektive und ihre Steigerungsformen anzuwenden
- Adverbien im Satz einzubetten
- Possessivpronomen anzuwenden
- das Present Perfect als weitere Zeitform zu nutzen
- Mengenangaben zu machen
- Will-Future und Going-to-Future richtig anzuwenden
- If-Satz Typ I zu bilden.

2.3 Inklusion und Lernen

Inklusion und Lernen im fremdsprachlichen Unterricht stellen oft eine große Herausforde-

2. Methodisch-didaktische Hinweise

rung für Lehrkräfte dar. Dieses Übungsbuch bietet Möglichkeiten, strukturierten Englischunterricht in Inklusionsklassen zu vereinfachen und auf die heterogenen Lernniveaus der Schülerinnen und Schüler auszurichten. Hauptaugenmerk ist hierbei, den Lehrkräften Materialien an die Hand zu geben und im Rahmen der Inklusion Übungsvarianten zu finden, die passend für alle Lernenden aufbereitet werden können. Dabei sind die wichtigsten Themen der englischen Grammatik für den 6. Jahrgang übersichtlich dargestellt und grundlegende Einzelaspekte hervorgehoben. Der Englischunterricht kann individuell dem jeweiligen Lernniveau angepasst werden, indem die Lernenden zwar gleiche Aufgaben erledigen, diese allerdings unterschiedliche Schwierigkeitsgrade aufweisen. Die Aufgaben für Lernschwache bieten hierbei besondere Unterstützung und Anleitung. Viele Illustrationen helfen zudem beim Verständnis der Aufgaben und fördern eine selbstständige Ausführung. Diese Form der Aufgaben ist besonders für Förderschüler und -schülerinnen zugänglich, da bei allen Übungen handlungsorientiertes Arbeiten und Lernen im Vordergrund steht.

2.4 Zu den Übungen

Lehrkräften bietet das Übungsbuch eine Bandbreite unterschiedlicher und leistungsdifferenzierter Übungen und somit die Möglichkeit, schnell und einfach Differenzierungsmaterial zu finden und auf die Lerngruppe (zielgleich/zieldifferent) abzustimmen. Die enthaltenen Kopiervorlagen können unterschiedlich zu den Themen des Lehrwerks eingesetzt werden. Sowohl lernstarke als auch lernschwache Schülerinnen und Schüler bearbeiten die gleichen Aufgaben, die zwar mit unterschiedlichen Anleitungen versehen sind, allerdings zu gleichen Ergebnissen führen. Auf diese Weise ist eine einheitliche Sicherung gewährleistet. Dies bedeutet konkret, dass Lehrkräfte für ihren Unterricht gezielt Themen aussuchen und differentes Lern- und Übungsmaterial schnell und einfach ergänzen können. Selbstverständlich können die Lernenden mit Förderbedarf auch die anspruchsvolleren Übungen bearbeiten, insbesondere, wenn sie ihre individuellen Arbeitsmaterialien zufriedenstellend erledigt haben und eine weitere Vertiefung gewünscht ist. Im digitalen Zusatzmaterial finden Sie zudem alle Lösungen zu den Aufgaben.

2.5 Merkmale auf einen Blick

- Abdeckung aller schulrelevanten Themen der englischen Grammatik in der 6. Jahrgangsstufe
- systematische Wiederholung und Festigung von Grundstoff
- einfache und klare Strukturierung
- kleinschrittige und vereinfachte Aufgaben
- differenziertes Übungsmaterial, sowohl für den regulären als auch für den Unterricht in Inklusionsklassen (geeignet für Lernende mit Förderbedarf)
- ermöglicht selbstständiges Arbeiten
- zweisprachige Arbeitsaufträge für Lernende mit sonderpädagogischem Förderbedarf
- unterstützende Illustrationen
- Grammatik schnell erklärt durch „Grammar Box"

Bedeutung der Aufgabennummerierung

① Aufgaben mit dieser Markierung sind für Regelschüler und -schülerinnen konzipiert worden, das heißt für Lernende, die nach den Anforderungen der allgemeinen Schule unterrichtet und bewertet werden. Sie orientieren sich an den allgemeingültigen Kompetenzen für den Englischunterricht.

❷ Aufgaben mit dieser Markierung sind für Förderschüler und -schülerinnen entwickelt worden, das heißt für Lernende mit sonderpädagogischem Förderbedarf, die zieldifferent unterrichtet werden.

Revision Grammar I

Grammar Box: Simple Present

- Das Simple Present verwendest du, um auszudrücken, wie häufig du etwas machst.
- Signalwörter dafür sind *usually, sometimes, always, often, never, every day/week/year/Monday/…*
- Beachte, dass bei der Form von *he/she/it* das Verb immer mit einem *-s* ergänzt wird!

  Bei Verben, die auf *-o, -sh, -ch* enden, wird ein *-es* angehängt.
  (*go – goes / do – does / watch – watches / finish – finishes*)

   MERKE ALSO → HE, SHE, IT, DAS „S" MUSS MIT!

- Merke dir auch die Sonderform des Verbs *have*.

I have	we have
you have	you have
he/she/it has	they have

- Wenn das Verb auf *-y* endet, dann wird das *-y* in der 3. Person Singular zu *-ie*. (*tidy – tidies*)

- Die **Verneinung** der Sätze im Simple Present erfolgt mit *don't* oder *doesn't*.
  → I don't go to school.
  → She doesn't go to school.

- **Fragen** werden mit *do* oder *does* gebildet.
  → Do you go to school?
  → Does she go to school?

- **Fragewörter** stehen am Anfang.
  → When do you go to school?
  → When do you eat breakfast?
  → Where do they meet?
  → What does she do?

Simple Present: Aussagen (1)

① **Put in the right verb form.**

1. Charly _____ (do) his homework.

2. The girls _____ (play) in the garden.

3. Monkeys _____ (love) bananas.

4. Mr Miller _____ (work) in the office.

5. He sometimes _____ (go) for a walk with the dog.

6. On Thursdays Sarah _____ (watch) TV with her mum.

7. I _____ (feed) the fish every day.

8. My parents _____ (travel) to Italy every summer.

9. My sisters _____ (help) dad in the garden.

10. The Millers _____ (have) a party every Saturday.

② **Put in the right verb.**

have (2x) • go • do • help • take • play • love • watch • visit

1. Sally and her friends _____ the animals in the zoo.

2. They always _____ the zoo in London.

3. Sally _____ TV in the afternoon.

4. Mrs Miller _____ the dog for a walk.

5. Ben _____ football with his friends.

6. Lisa _____ a lot of homework for school.

7. The students _____ projects for art club.

8. Jay _____ his mum in the kitchen.

9. Dave _____ to the cinema every Saturday.

10. Jennifer _____ her homework every day.

8

© PERSEN Verlag

Simple Present: Aussagen (2)

③ **What do you do in your free time? Write five sentences.**

I	go	football/tennis	on Mondays.
	listen to	shopping	every week.
	watch	TV	every Saturday.
	play	my homework	…
	do	music/the radio	

1. _____.
2. _____.
3. _____.
4. _____.
5. _____.

④ **Write what your best friend does on Sundays.**

He/She	get up	at eight o'clock.
	take a shower	at ten o'clock.
	have breakfast	in the afternoon.
	watch TV	in the evening.
	do some homework	in the morning.
	…	…

1. _____.
2. _____.
3. _____.
4. _____.
5. _____.

Simple Present: Aussagen (1)

❶ **Choose the right verb form.**
Wähle die passende Verbform.

1. **Charly** _____ (do/does) his homework.

2. **The girls** _____ (play/plays) in the garden.

3. **Monkeys** _____ (love/loves) bananas.

4. **Mr Miller** _____ (work/works) in the office.

5. **He** sometimes _____ (go/goes) for a walk with the dog.

6. On Thursdays **Sarah** _____ (watch/watches) TV with her mum.

7. **I** _____ (feed/feeds) the fish every day.

8. **My parents** _____ (travel/travels) to Italy every summer.

9. **My sisters** _____ (help/helps) dad in the garden.

10. **The Millers** _____ (have/has) a party every Saturday.

❷ **Put in the right form. Be careful with *he, she, it*!**
Setze die richtige Verbform ein. Achte auf die Besonderheit bei *he, she* und *it*!

1. Sally and her friends _____ (love) the animals in the zoo.

2. They always _____ (visit) the zoo in London.

3. Sally _____ (watch) TV in the afternoon.

4. Mrs Miller _____ (take) the dog for a walk.

5. Ben _____ (play) football with his friends.

6. Lisa _____ (have) a lot of homework for school.

7. The students _____ (have) projects for art club.

8. Jay _____ (help) his mum in the kitchen.

9. Dave _____ (go) to the cinema every Saturday.

10. Jennifer _____ (do) her homework every day.

Simple Present: Aussagen (2)

❸ What do you do in your free time? Write five sentences.

Was tust du in deiner Freizeit? Verbinde zu fünf sinnvollen Sätzen.

I	go	shopping	on Mondays.
	listen to	music	every week.
	watch	TV	every Saturday.
	play	football	…
	do	my homework	

1. _____.
2. _____.
3. _____.
4. _____.
5. _____.

❹ Write what your best friend does on Sundays.

Schreibe auf, was dein bester Freund/deine beste Freundin am Sonntag macht.

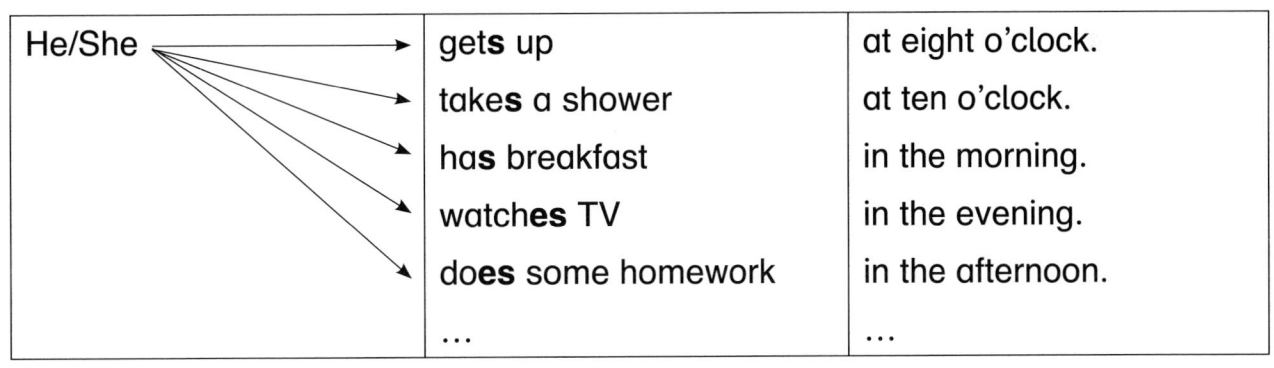

He/She	gets up	at eight o'clock.
	takes a shower	at ten o'clock.
	has breakfast	in the morning.
	watches TV	in the evening.
	does some homework	in the afternoon.
	…	…

1. _____.
2. _____.
3. _____.
4. _____.
5. _____.

Simple Present: Verneinung

① **Put in *don't* or *doesn't*.**

1. Monkeys _____ eat apples, they eat bananas.

2. Students _____ stay at home in the morning because they go to school.

3. Teachers _____ teach teachers. They teach students.

4. Animals _____ play football. They just walk in their cages.

5. The girl _____ look sad, she is happy.

6. My mother _____ cook in the bathroom. She cooks in the kitchen.

② **Look at the pictures and make sentences.**

1. 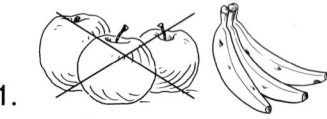 Sally (bananas – apples) / like

   Sally doesn't like apples. She likes bananas.

2.  Mr Miller (spaghetti – pizza) / eat

   _____ .

3. 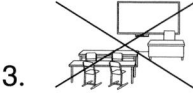 students (playground – classrom) / play

   _____ .

4. 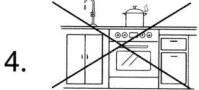 Ben (bike – kitchen) / clean

   _____ .

5.  Jason (cat – dog) / feed

   _____ .

6.  Sarah (tennis – football) / play

   _____ .

Simple Present: Verneinung

❶ Circle the right form.

Kreise das richtige Wort ein.

1. Monkeys **don't** or doesn't eat apples, they eat bananas.

2. Students don't or doesn't stay at home in the morning because they go to school.

3. Teachers don't or doesn't teach teachers. They teach students.

4. Animals don't or doesn't play football. They just walk in their cages.

5. The girl don't or doesn't look sad, she is happy.

6. My mother don't or doesn't cook in the bathroom. She cooks in the kitchen.

❷ Look at the pictures and make sentences.

Schau dir die Bilder an und bilde Sätze.

1.  Sally (bananas – apples) / like   doesn't like – likes

   Sally doesn't like apples. She likes bananas.

2. Mr Miller (spaghetti – pizza) / eat   doesn't eat – eats

   _____.

3.  students (playground – classrom) / play   don't play – play

   _____.

4.  Ben (bike – kitchen) / clean   doesn't clean – cleans

   _____.

5.  Jason (cat – dog) / feed   doesn't feed – feeds

   _____.

6.  Sarah (tennis – football) / play   doesn't play – plays

   _____.

Simple Present: Fragen

① **Answer these questions.**

1. When do you go to school?
   _____.

2. What does your mother cook?
   _____.

3. When does school finish?
   _____.

4. Do you like pets?
   _____.

5. Does your best friend have a pet?
   _____.

6. Where do you live?
   _____.

② **Write down the questions – use question words!**

1. Sally gets up **at seven o'clock.**
   _____.

2. She has breakfast **at home.**
   _____.

3. My friend's name is **Leo.**
   _____.

4. My books are **on my desk.**
   _____.

5. The animals love **food.**
   _____.

6. **My mother** cleans the kitchen.
   _____.

Simple Present: Fragen

❶ Answer these questions.

Beantworte die Fragen.

1. When do you go to school? Wann gehst du zur Schule?

   _____.

2. What does your mother cook? Was kocht deine Mama?

   _____.

3. When does school finish? Wann endet die Schule?

   _____.

4. Do you like pets? Magst du Tiere?

   _____.

5. Does your best friend have a pet? Hat dein bester Freund ein Haustier?

   _____.

6. Where do you live? Wo lebst du?

   _____.

❷ Write down the questions.

Notiere die Fragen zu den Antworten.

1. Sally gets up **at seven o'clock**.

   When _____?

2. She has breakfast **at home**.

   Where _____?

3. My friend's name is **Leo**.

   What's _____?

4. My books are **on my desk**.

   Where _____?

5. The animals love **food**.

   What _____?

6. My mother cleans **the kitchen**.

   What _____?

Revision Grammar II

Grammar Box: Simple Past

Du verwendest das Simple Past, um auszudrücken, was geschehen ist.

Signalwörter sind: *yesterday, last week, last year, last Monday, two days ago ...*

Die Bildung des Simple Past erfolgt durch das Anhängen von *-ed* an das Verb. Aber Achtung! Das kannst du nur bei **regelmäßigen Verben** machen. Die **unregelmäßigen Verben** musst du lernen.

Anders als im Deutschen gibt es im Englischen nur die Verwendung des Simple Past, um Vergangenes, das zu einem bestimmten Zeitpunkt stattgefunden hat, auszudrücken.

play → play**ed** → I played basketball yesterday.

Ich spielte gestern Basketball. / Ich habe gestern Basketball gespielt.

watch → watch**ed** → I watched TV last weekend.

Ich schaute letztes Wochenende Fernsehen. / Ich habe letztes Wochenende ferngesehen.

 Merke dir die Schreibweise bei folgenden Verben:

➜ Verdopplung des Konsonanten nach kurzem Vokal am Wortende

stop → sto**pp**ed   clap → cla**pp**ed   rob → ro**bb**ed   travel → trave**ll**ed

➜ *-y* nach Konsonant wird zu *-ied*

carry → carr**ied**   hurry → hurr**ied**

➜ Das stumme *-e* am Ende entfällt

love → loved

Fragen

Die Fragen im Simple Past bildest du ebenfalls mit *did*.

Did you go to school yesterday? – No, because I was ill.

Did she go to the cinema last week? – No, her friends didn't have time.

Fragewörter stehen am Anfang!

When did you come home?

Why did you come late?

What did you buy?

Verneinung

Die Verneinung im Simple Past wird mit *didn't* gebildet.

Did you watch TV? No, I didn't (watch TV).

Did she watch TV? – No, she didn't (watch TV).

Simple Past: Aussagen (1)

① **Find the words and then make sentences.**

Q	S	D	M	P	I	G	R	M	K	E	Z	Y	E	X	U	W	R	F	G	I	P	S	M	L	H
F	A	W	A	N	T	E	D	N	A	T	I	S	I	M	S	K	F	E	L	O	G	R	A	D	T
D	M	I	K	A	E	O	P	F	E	N	I	C	S	Y	N	G	H	O	M	N	F	I	E	H	Z
U	A	B	J	R	M	A	I	A	P	L	A	Y	E	D	O	Q	S	J	U	N	I	K	T	O	O
Y	I	O	V	D	A	X	O	N	S	D	N	I	X	Y	T	H	L	G	N	E	N	A	E	S	W
U	Y	I	E	E	L	X	N	K	W	J	G	W	M	B	T	K	V	U	O	F	I	L	M	A	A
W	S	W	A	T	C	H	E	D	T	A	O	O	H	O	I	L	A	L	P	E	S	E	P	S	L
O	C	Y	N	N	A	U	M	L	I	R	N	R	E	L	N	I	T	C	H	S	H	T	U	I	K
N	S	I	T	W	L	S	A	J	O	A	M	K	N	A	O	S	E	H	I	T	E	H	R	N	E
M	X	P	H	A	L	B	W	W	N	N	E	E	P	J	V	T	O	L	C	O	D	I	A	D	D
A	T	P	Y	E	E	A	K	Y	R	L	C	D	H	R	A	E	T	O	A	N	P	O	R	R	K
B	H	E	R	L	D	S	Y	N	D	A	H	S	I	U	G	N	J	P	L	Y	A	N	I	A	I
I	O	N	J	D	R	T	R	M	M	D	C	L	E	A	N	E	D	H	I	K	N	W	S	G	A
K	T	E	M	P	Z	E	I	R	A	L	O	H	G	I	K	D	K	A	S	A	L	O	G	I	N

1. Amber _____ to music.
2. She _____ her project work for school.
3. Her dad _____ in the office yesterday.
4. Her sister _____ with her friends in the garden.
5. Later she _____ the dog in the park.
6. Her mother _____ to do the shopping and _____ the kitchen.
7. In the evening they _____ TV.
8. She _____ her friends.

② **Fill in the chart with the missing verbs. Have a look at the list of irregular verbs.**

infinitive	simple past	German translation
buy	bought	kaufen
wear		
	saw	
	taught	
bring		
		nehmen
eat		
	fed	

Simple Past: Aussagen (2)

③ **Put in the verbs to complete the sentences. What did they all do? Use the simple past forms.**

eat • clean • repair • buy • go • play

1. Julia _____ to the cinema with her friends.

2. Sarah and Ben _____ two T-shirts last Tuesday.

3. David _____ his bike.

4. The friends _____ football.

5. Tim _____ his room.

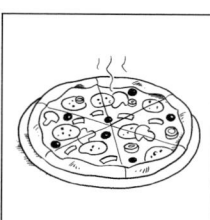

6. Sandra and Lucy _____ pizza.

④ **Which word is wrong?**

1. go – talked – saw – ran
2. listened – walked – write – bought
3. wanted – do – had – put
4. talked – went – like – did

Simple Past: Aussagen (3)

⑤ **Match the sentences.**

1. Mum and Dad went to the restaurant.	a) She watched the same movie as me.
2. Sarah went shopping.	b) She got many presents.
3. Deborah invited her friends to her birthday party.	c) They talked about their problems.
4. Lucy called her friend Sarah.	d) She bought some clothes.
5. Charlie had a match last weekend.	e) They ate pizza.
6. I met Sarah at the cinema.	f) He was happy because they won the match.

⑥ **We don't understand German. Translate the sentences.**

1. Er traf seine Freunde im Kino.

   _____

2. Die Freunde aßen Pizza.

   _____

3. Die Nachbarn hatten eine große Torte für die Party.

   _____

4. Er fuhr mit seinem Fahrrad nach Hause.

   _____

⑦ **The simple past snake – find the forms.**

Simple Past: Aussagen (1)

❶ **Find the words and then make sentences.**

Finde die Wörter und bilde daraus Sätze.

Q	S	D	M	P	I	G	R	M	K	E	Z	Y	E	X	U	W	R	F	G	I	P	S	M	L	H
F	A	W	A	N	T	E	D	N	A	T	I	S	I	M	S	K	F	E	L	O	G	R	A	D	T
D	M	I	K	A	E	O	P	F	E	N	I	C	S	Y	N	G	H	O	M	N	F	I	E	H	Z
U	A	B	J	R	M	A	I	A	P	L	A	Y	E	D	O	Q	S	J	U	N	I	K	T	O	O
Y	I	O	V	D	A	X	O	N	S	D	N	I	X	Y	T	H	L	G	N	E	N	A	E	S	W
U	Y	I	E	E	L	X	N	K	W	J	G	W	M	B	T	K	V	U	O	F	I	L	M	A	A
W	S	W	A	T	C	H	E	D	T	A	O	O	H	O	I	L	A	L	P	E	S	E	P	S	L
O	C	Y	N	N	A	U	M	L	I	R	N	R	E	L	N	I	T	C	H	S	H	T	U	I	K
N	S	I	T	W	L	S	A	J	O	A	M	K	N	A	O	S	E	H	I	T	E	H	R	N	E
M	X	P	H	A	L	B	W	W	N	N	E	E	P	J	V	T	O	L	C	O	D	I	A	D	D
A	T	P	Y	E	E	A	K	Y	R	L	C	D	H	R	A	E	T	O	A	N	P	O	R	R	K
B	H	E	R	L	D	S	Y	N	D	A	H	S	I	U	G	N	J	P	L	Y	A	N	I	A	I
I	O	N	J	D	R	T	R	M	M	D	C	L	E	A	N	E	D	H	I	K	N	W	S	G	A
K	T	E	M	P	Z	E	I	R	A	L	O	H	G	I	K	D	K	A	S	A	L	O	G	I	N

1. Amber **listened** to music. (listen)
2. She _____ her project work for school. (finish)
3. Her dad _____ in the office yesterday. (work)
4. Her sister _____ with her friends in the garden. (play)
5. Later she _____ the dog in the park. (walk)
6. Her mother _____ to do the shopping and _____ the kitchen. (want/clean)
7. In the evening they _____ TV. (watch)
8. She _____ her friends. (call)

❷ **Fill in the chart with the missing verbs. Have a look at the list of irregular verbs.**

Vervollständige die Tabelle. Die Vokabelliste kann dich unterstützen.

infinitive	simple past	German translation
buy	bought	kaufen
wear	_____	tragen
_____	saw	sehen

Simple Past: Aussagen (2)

infinitive	simple past	German translation
_ _ _ _ _ _	taught	unterrichten, lehren
bring	_ _ _ _ _ _ _ _	bringen
take	_ _ _ _ _	nehmen
eat	_ _ _ _	essen
_ _ _ _ _	fed	füttern

③ Fill in the simple past forms to complete the sentences. What did they all do?

Vervollständige die Sätze mit der richtigen Form im Simple Past. Was haben die Personen alle gemacht?

1. Julia _____ to the cinema with her friends. (go)

2. Sarah and Ben _____ two T-shirts last Tuesday. (buy)

3. David _____ his bike. (repair)

4. The friends _____ football. (play)

Simple Past: Aussagen (3)

4 **Which word is wrong? Cross it out.**

Welche Form ist falsch? Streiche durch.

1. **go** – talked – saw – ran
2. listened – walked – **write** – bought
3. wanted – **do** – had – put
4. talked – went – **like** – did

5 **Match the sentences.**

Verbinde die Sätze passend. Achte auf die fett gedruckten Begriffe. Sie helfen dir dabei, die Sätze zu verbinden.

1. Mum and Dad went to the **restaurant**.
2. Sarah went **shopping**.
3. Deborah invited her friends to her **birthday party**.
4. Lucy **called** her friend Sarah.
5. Charlie had a **match** last weekend.
6. I met Sarah at the **cinema**.

a) She watched the same **movie**.
b) She got many **presents**.
c) They **talked** about their problems.
d) She bought some **clothes**.
e) They ate **pizza**.
f) He was happy because they won the **match**.

1	2	3	4	5	6
e					

Simple Past: Aussagen (4)

❻ We don't understand German. Translate the following sentences.

Wir verstehen kein Deutsch. Übersetze die Sätze und entscheide dich für die richtige Form.

1. Er traf seine Freunde im Kino. (he / meet – met / his friends / at the cinema)

   _____

2. Die Freunde aßen Pizza. (the friends / eat – ate / pizza)

   _____

3. Die Nachbarn hatten eine große Party. (the neighbours / have – had / a big party)

   _____

4. Er fuhr mit seinem Fahrrad nach Hause. (he / his bike / ride – rode / home)

   _____

❼ The simple past snake – find the forms.

Finde die Simple Past-Formen in der Schlange.

Simple Past: Verneinung (1)

① **Put the words in the right order and make correct sentences.**

1. didn't – to school – go – Sally

____

2. play – the students – didn't – football – after school

____

3. my friends – see – the afternoon – in – I – didn't

____

4. David – swimming – go – didn't

____

5. eat – in the cafeteria – the friends – didn't – lunch

____

6. my mum – go shopping – didn't – yesterday

____

② **Have a look at the pictures and write down what happened or what didn't happen yesterday.**

1

3

2

4

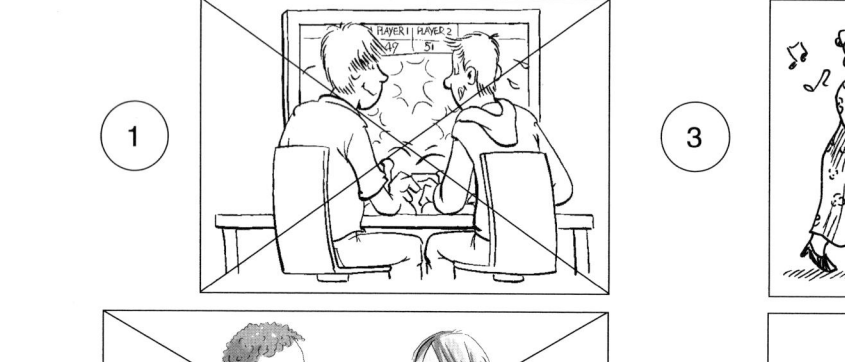

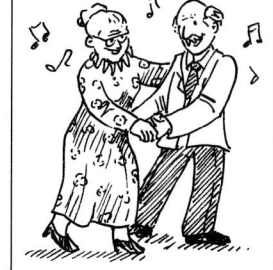

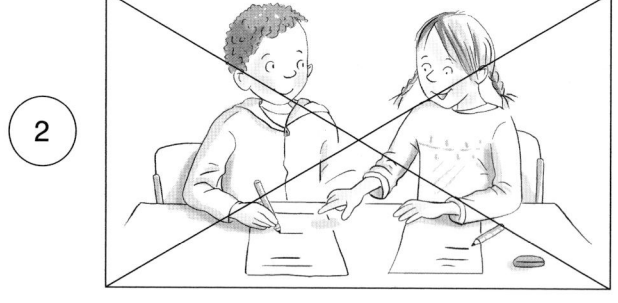

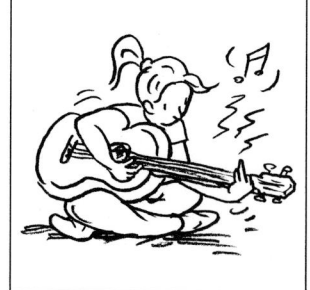

1. The boys ____.
2. The kids ____.
3. The grandparents ____.
4. The girl ____.

Simple Past: Verneinung (2)

③ **John went to Italy with his parents. David stayed at home.**
Write down what David didn't do.

1. John went to Italy.

   David _____.

2. John walked along the beach.

   _____.

3. John ate a lot of ice cream.

   _____.

4. John met new friends.

   _____.

④ **What did you do yesterday? What didn't you do yesterday?**
Write down 4 sentences.

1. _____

2. _____

3. _____

4. _____

Simple Past: Verneinung (1)

❶ **Put the words in the right order.**

Bringe die Wörter in die richtige Reihenfolge. Setze zunächst die Ziffern. Schreibe dann den Satz richtig auf.

1. didn't ( ) – to school. ( ) – go ( ) – **Sally (1)**

   Sally _____

2. play ( ) – **The students (1)** – didn't ( ) – football ( ) – after school. ( )

   _____

3. my friends ( ) – see ( ) – the afternoon. ( ) – in ( ) – **I (1)** – didn't ( )

   _____

4. **David (1)** – swimming. ( ) – go ( ) – didn't ( )

   _____

5. eat ( ) – in the cafeteria. ( ) – **The friends (1)** – didn't ( ) – lunch ( )

   _____

6. **My mum (1)** – go shopping ( ) – didn't ( ) – yesterday. ( )

   _____

❷ **Have a look at the pictures. What happened and what didn't happen yesterday? Connect the pictures with the sentences.**

Schau dir die Bilder an. Was ist gestern passiert und was nicht? Ordne die Sätze den Bildern zu.

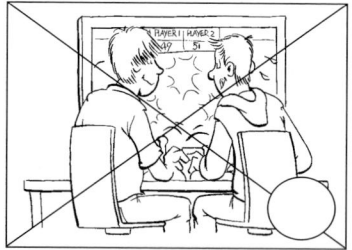   

1. The boys didn't play computer games.
2. The kids didn't do their homework.
3. The grandparents danced and sang.
4. The girl played the guitar.

Simple Past: Verneinung (2)

**❸ John went to Italy with his parents.
David stayed at home.
Combine the sentences correctly.**

John hat die Ferien mit seinen Eltern in Italien verbracht.
David hat die Ferien zu Hause verbracht.
Verbinde die Sätze richtig.

John went to Italy.	David didn't eat a lot of ice cream.
John walked along the beach.	David didn't meet new friends.
John ate a lot of ice cream.	David didn't walk along the beach.
John met new friends.	David didn't go to Italy.

**❹ What did you do yesterday? What didn't you do yesterday?
Write down 4 sentences.
Use the ideas in the box.**

Was hast du gestern gemacht und was hast du nicht gemacht?
Notiere 4 Sätze (2 mit *did* und 2 mit *didn't*).
Verwende die Ideen aus der Box.

> do homework • ride my bike • finish the painting • do the shopping •
> repair the bike • wash dad's car • watch TV • play games • go swimming

1. _____
2. _____
3. _____
4. _____

Simple Past: Fragen (1)

① **Write down five question words. They start with *wh*.**

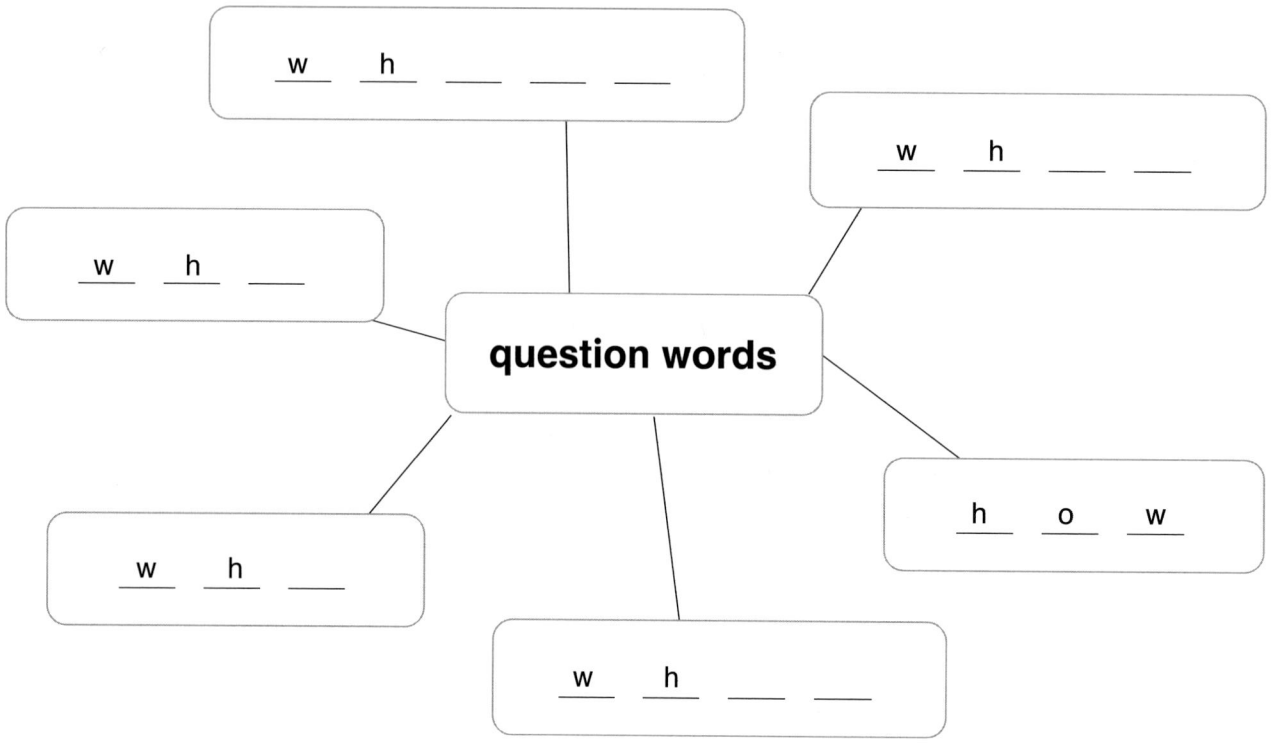

② **Fill in the question words.**

1. _____ did you eat? Chocolate and sweets.

2. _____ did you go? I went to the cinema.

3. _____ did you watch? I watched a movie.

4. _____ did you go there? I went there by bike.

5. _____ did you meet your friends? I met my friends in the afternoon.

6. _____ is your Maths teacher? It is Mrs Miller.

Simple Past: Fragen (2)

③ **Tick the right answer.**

1.	Where did you go last holidays?	☐ I wrote my homework.
		☑ I went to Italy.
2.	When did you come back?	☐ Two days ago.
		☐ I stayed two weeks.
3.	What did you do in Italy?	☐ I did many activities.
		☐ I stayed at home.
4.	How did you go there?	☐ I went there by plane.
		☐ I stayed with my family.

④ **Have a look at the pictures and write down the questions.**

The boy played **in the park**.

Lucy did **her homework**.

They played **football**.

The party was **last weekend**.

He stayed **in a hotel**.

They cleaned **the kitchen**.

Simple Past: Fragen (3)

⑤ Find the right answers and fill in the chart. There are always two answers possible.

1. Did you find your books?	a) Yes, I did.
2. Did your sisters pack their sandwiches?	b) No, I didn't.
3. Did your friends go shopping?	c) Yes, they did.
4. Did David go with his parents?	d) No, he didn't.
5. Did Tom clean his room?	e) Yes, he did.
6. Did you send a nice postcard to grandad?	f) No, they didn't.

1	2	3	4	5	6
a + b					

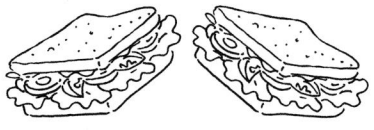

⑥ Answer the questions below. (Yes, I did. / No, I didn't.)

1. Did you go to the cinema last weekend? _____

2. Did you watch a funny movie with your friends? _____

3. Did you tidy up your room? _____

4. Did you help your mum in the kitchen? _____

5. Did you repair your brother's bike? _____

6. Did you go to school on Sunday? _____

Simple Past: Fragen (4)

Now ask your partner questions and write down his or her answers.

1. Did you … _____ ?
   _____

2. _____ ?
   _____

3. _____ ?
   _____

4. _____ ?
   _____

5. _____ ?
   _____

6. _____ ?
   _____

⑦ **Put the words in the right order and make questions.**

1. Ben – did – when – go – to the park – ?
   _____

2. when – Sally – visit – grandma – her – did – ?
   _____

3. Lucy – in the restaurant – eat – and her mum – what – did – ?
   _____

4. did – a movie – watch – Oliver – ?
   _____

5. in the garden – did – he – with his friends – play – ?
   _____

6. what – did – eat – they – for lunch – ?
   _____

Simple Past: Fragen (1)

❶ **Write down the five missing question words: what · where · when · why · who.**
   Schreibe die fünf fehlenden Fragewörter (what · where · when · why · who) auf.
   Achte auf die Buchstabenanzahl!

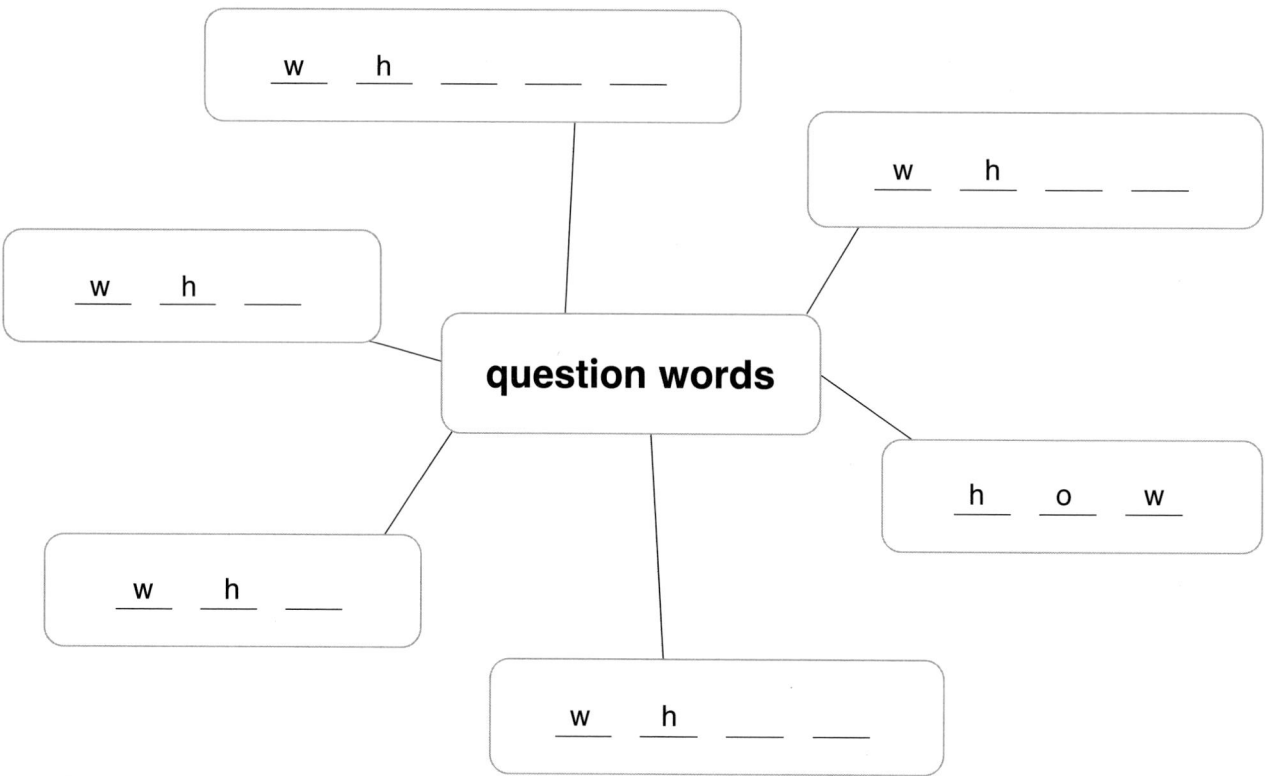

❷ **Fill in the question words.**
   Setze die Fragewörter ein.

1. _ _ _ _ did you eat? Chocolate and sweets. (Was)

2. _ _ _ _ _ did you go? I went to the cinema. (Wo/Wohin)

3. _ _ _ _ did you watch? I watched a movie. (Was)

4. _ _ _ did you go there? I went there by bike. (Wie)

5. _ _ _ _ did you meet your friends? I met them in the afternoon. (Wann)

Simple Past: Fragen (2)

❸ Tick the right answer.

Setze ein Häkchen bei der richtigen Antwort.

1.	Where did you go last holidays? Wo/Wohin …	☐ I wrote my homework. ☑ I went to Italy.
2.	When did you come back? Wann …	☐ Two days ago. ☐ I stayed two weeks.
3.	What did you do in Italy? Was …	☐ I did many activities. ☐ I stayed at home.
4.	How did you go there? Wie …	☐ I went there by plane. ☐ I stayed with my family.

❹ Have a look at the pictures and write the questions.

Schau dir die Bilder an und notiere die richtigen Fragen.

Where _____

_____

The boy played **in the park**.

What _____

_____

Lucy did **her homework**.

What _____

_____

They played **football**.

When _____

_____

The party was **last weekend**.

Where _____

_____

He stayed **in a hotel**.

What _____

_____

They cleaned **the kitchen**.

Simple Past: Fragen (3)

❺ Find the right answers and match the sentences. You can use different colours. There are always two answers possible.

**Verbinde die richtigen Antworten und trage die Buchstaben in die Tabelle ein. Du kannst verschiedene Farben verwenden.
Es sind immer zwei Antworten richtig.**

1. Did **you (I)** find your books?
2. Did **your sisters (they)** pack their sandwiches?
3. Did **your friends (they)** go shopping?
4. Did **David (he)** go with his parents?
5. Did **you (I)** clean your room?
6. Did **your brother (he)** send a nice postcard to grandad?

a) Yes, **he** did.
b) No, **I** didn't.
c) Yes, **they** did.
d) No, **he** didn't.
e) Yes, **I** did.
f) No, **they** didn't.

1	2	3	4	5	6
b + e					

**❻ Answer the questions below with „Yes, I did." or „No, I didn't."!
Just circle the right answer.**

**Beantworte die Fragen mit „Yes, I did." oder „No, I didn't."!
Kreise deine Antwort ein.**

1. Did you go to the cinema last weekend? Yes, I did. / No, I didn't.
2. Did you watch a funny movie with your friends? Yes, I did. / No, I didn't.
3. Did you tidy up your room? Yes, I did. / No, I didn't.
4. Did you help your mum in the kitchen? Yes, I did. / No, I didn't.
5. Did you repair your bike? Yes, I did. / No, I didn't.
6. Did you go to school on Sunday? Yes, I did. / No, I didn't.

Simple Past: Fragen (4)

Now ask your partner questions and write down his or her answers. Use the ideas in the box.

Stelle deinem Partner oder deiner Partnerin Fragen und notiere die Antworten. Du kannst auch die Ideen in der Box nutzen.

Did you …	… eat many sweets?
	… ride your bike in the park?
	… take the dog for a walk?
	… travel to Italy with your family?
	… help your father in the garden?
	… have a birthday party last year?

1. Did you _____?

   _____

2. _____?

   _____

3. _____?

   _____

4. _____?

   _____

5. _____?

   _____

6. _____?

Simple Past: Fragen (5)

❼ Put the words in the right order and make questions.

Bringe die Wörter in die richtige Reihenfolge. Schreibe die Zahlen der richtigen Reihenfolge in die Klammern. Schreibe dann die vollständigen Fragen auf.

1. Ben (3) – did (2) – **When (1)** – go (4) – to the park? (5)

   When did Ben go to the park?

2. **When (1)** – Sally ( ) – visit ( ) – grandma? ( ) – her ( ) – did ( )

   _____

3. Lucy ( ) – in the restaurant? ( ) – eat ( ) – and her mum ( ) – **What (1)** – did ( )

   _____

4. **Did (1)** – a movie? ( ) – watch ( ) – Oliver ( )

   _____

5. in the garden ( ) – **Did (1)** – he ( ) – with his friends? ( ) – play ( )

   _____

6. **What (1)** – did ( ) – eat ( ) – they ( ) – for lunch? ( )

   _____

Revision Grammar III

Grammar Box: Das Verb *to be*

Du weißt bereits, dass das Verb *to be* „sein" bedeutet.
Ähnlich wie im Deutschen ist das Verb unregelmäßig.

to be im Simple Present

long form	short form	Verneinung long form	Verneinung short form
I am	I'm	I am not	I'm not
you are	you're	you are not	you aren't
he/she/it is	he's/she's/it's	he/she/it is not	he's not/she's not/it's not
we are	we're	we are not	we aren't
you are	you're	you are not	you aren't
they are	they're	they are not	they aren't

to be im Simple Past

long form	short form	Verneinung long form	Verneinung short form
I was	–	I was not	I wasn't
you were	–	you were not	you weren't
he/she/it was	–	he/she/it was not	he/she/it wasn't
we were	–	we were not	we weren't
you were	–	you were not	you weren't
they were	–	they were not	they weren't

To be: Übungen (1)

① **Fill in the simple present and simple past forms of *to be*.**

simple present

1. It ***is*** a big show.
2. I _____ ten years old.
3. She _____ a nice girl.
4. We _____ at home.
5. They _____ at school.
6. You _____ a good student.

simple past

It ***was*** a big show.
I _____ ten years old.
She _____ a nice girl.
We _____ at home.
They _____ at school.
You _____ a good student.

② **Find the simple present and simple past forms of *to be* and write them down.**

a)

aregbbiamhikuarealisaruarebbiarefg

I _____	we _____
you _____	you _____
he/she/it _____	they _____

b)

werekgiweredaiwaskwerebiaywasiigkweredq

I _____	we _____
you _____	you _____
he/she/it _____	they _____

To be: Übungen (2)

c) **Write sentences with the simple present and simple past forms of *to be*.**

simple present

1. _____
2. _____
3. _____
4. _____
5. _____

simple past

1. _____
2. _____
3. _____
4. _____
5. _____

simple present
am is are

simple past
was were

To be: Übungen (1)

**❶ Fill in the simple present and simple past forms of *to be*.
Use the grammar box as help.**

**Vervollständige die Präsens- und Vergangenheitsformen.
Die Grammar Box kann dir helfen.**

simple present	simple past
1. It *is* a big show.	1. It **was** a big show.
2. I _____ ten years old.	2. I _____ ten years old.
3. She _____ a nice girl.	3. She _____ a nice girl.
4. We _____ at home.	4. We _____ at home.
5. They _____ at school.	5. They _____ at school.
6. You _____ a good student.	6. You _____ a good student.

❷ Find the simple present and the simple past forms of *to be* and write them down.

Finde die richtige Präsens- (simple present) und Präteritumsform (simple past) von *to be* und notiere sie.

a)

aregbamhk**are**alisqr**are**bi**are**

I __ __   we __ __ __

you __ __ __   you __ __ __

he/she/it __ __   they __ __ __

To be: Übungen (2)

b)

werekiwerediwaskllwerebywasigkwere

I _ _ _		we _ _ _ _
you _ _ _ _		you _ _ _ _
he/she/it _ _ _		they _ _ _ _

c) **Write sentences with the simple present and simple past forms of *to be*. Use the ideas in brackets.**

Schreibe Sätze im Präsens (simple present) und im Präteritum (simple past). Nutze die Ideen in den Klammern.

simple present

(*I – at home – with the dog / She – a very – good dancer*)

1. _____

2. _____

simple past

(*My little sister – very quiet – yesterday / You – my best friend*)

1. _____

2. _____

Grammar Mix: Simple Past vs. Simple Present (1)

① **Put in the simple past form.**

Last evening I _____ (go) to bed late. I _____ (be) really tired because I _____ (play) computer games. This morning I _____ _____ (wake up) very late. First I _____ (have) breakfast with my mum. She _____ (drink) coffee and we _____ (eat) bagels. Then I _____ (clean) my room and _____ (go) for a walk with the dog. In the park I _____ (meet) Toby. We _____ (ride) our bikes home and _____ (watch) a movie. That _____ (be) really scary.

② **Complete the dialogue.**

Cathreen: Hi, Simon! How are you? _____ (do) you do homework for Maths yesterday?

Simon: No, I _____ (not do). I _____ _____ (not have) time.

Cathreen: Oh, ok, but what _____ (do) you do all the time?

Simon: I _____ (have) to clean my bike and I _____ (help) my dad. We _____ (clean) the kitchen because my mum _____ (be) ill. What _____ (do) you do?

Cathreen: I _____ (go) to the shopping centre. I _____ (buy) some clothes and later I _____ (do) the Maths homework. That _____ (be) really difficult and it _____ (take) a lot of time.

③ **What about your weekend? Write down questions and ask your partner about his or her weekend.**

1. Where _____ ?
2. When _____ ?
3. What _____ ?
4. Why _____ ?

Grammar Mix: Simple Past vs. Simple Present (2)

④ **Signal words – simple present or simple past? Fill in the table.**

often • yesterday • sometimes • always • last week • usually • last year • two days ago • never • last Monday

simple present	simple past

⑤ **At the zoo**

Simple present or simple past? Fill in the right forms. Be careful with the tenses.

Yesterday I _____ (go) to the zoo with my parents. There _____ (be) many animals.

You can _____ (visit) the zoo every day. It _____ (open) at 10 o'clock in the morning.

First I _____ (see) the elephants. They _____ (be) so big.

Then I _____ (go) to the lions and something _____ (happen) at their cage.

One of the lions _____ (get) a baby. It _____ (look) so sweet and small. I really _____ (enjoy) that day. Today I _____ (stay) at home and I _____ (watch) TV with my parents.

Grammar Mix: Simple Past vs. Simple Present (1)

❶ Put in the simple past form. Choose the right form from the box.
Setze die Vergangenheitsform ein. Wähle die richtige Form aus der Box aus.

> went • ate • played • woke up • was • drank • cleaned • went • rode •
> watched • met • was • had

Last evening I _____ (go) to bed late. I _____ (be) really tired because I _____ (play) computer games. This morning I _____ _____ (wake up) very late. First I _____ (have) breakfast with my mum. She _____ (drink) coffee and we _____ (eat) bagels. Then I _____ (clean) my room and _____ (go) for a walk with the dog. In the park I _____ (meet) Toby. We _____ (ride) our bikes home and _____ (watch) a movie. That _____ (be) really scary.

❷ Complete the dialogue. The words in the box will help you.
Vervollständige den Dialog. Die Formen in der Box helfen dir dabei.

> bought • Did • didn't have • had • helped • cleaned • was • didn't •
> went • did • took • did • was • did

Cathreen: Hi, Simon! How are you? _____ (do) you do homework for Maths yesterday?

Simon: No, I _____ (not do). I _____ _____ (not have) time.

Cathreen: Oh, ok, but what _____ (do) you do all the time?

Simon: I _____ (have) to clean my bike and I _____ (help) my dad. We _____ (clean) the kitchen because my mum _____ (be) ill. What _____ (do) you do?

Cathreen: I _____ (go) to the shopping centre. I _____ (buy) some clothes and later I _____ (do) the Maths homework. That _____ (be) really difficult and it _____ (take) a lot of time.

Grammar Mix: Simple Past vs. Simple Present (2)

❸ **What about your weekend? Write down questions and ask your partner about his weekend.**

Wie war dein Wochende? Notiere Fragen und stelle sie deinem Partner.

1. Where did you _____?

2. When did _____?

3. What did _____?

4. Why _____?

❹ **Signal words – simple present or simple past? Fill in the chart.**

Signalwörter – folge den Ziffern und setze richtig ein.

often¹ • yesterday² • sometimes¹ • always¹ • last week² • usually¹ • last year² • two days ago² • never¹ • last Monday²

simple present¹	simple past²

❺ **Simple present or simple past? Fill in the right forms. Be careful with the tenses.**

Simple present oder simple past? Trage die richtigen Zeitformen in die Lücken ein. Achte dabei auf die Signalwörter.

Yesterday I _____ (go) to the zoo with my parents. There _____ (be) many animals. You can _____ (visit) the zoo **every day**. It _____ (open) at 10 o'clock in the morning. First I _____ (see) the elephants. They _____ (be) so big. Then I _____ (go) to the lions and something _____ (happen) at their cage. One of the lions _____ (get) a baby. It _____ (look) so sweet and small. I really _____ (enjoy) that day.

Today I _____ (stay) at home and I _____ (watch) TV with my parents.

Übersicht: Irregular verbs

infinitive	simple past	German
be	was, were	sein
become	became	werden
break	broke	brechen
bring	brought	bringen
buy	bought	kaufen
choose	chose	aussuchen, wählen
come	came	kommen
do	did	machen, tun
eat	ate	essen
fall	fell	fallen, hinfallen
feed	fed	füttern
find	found	finden
forget	forgot	vergessen
get	got	bekommen
give	gave	geben
go	went	gehen
have	had	haben
hear	heard	hören
know	knew	wissen
make	made	machen, tun
meet	met	treffen
put	put	stellen, legen, setzen
read	read	lesen
run	ran	laufen
say	said	sagen
see	saw	sehen
send	sent	verschicken, versenden
sing	sang	singen
sit	sat	sitzen
sleep	slept	schlafen
swim	swam	schwimmen
take	took	nehmen
teach	taught	unterrichten, lehren
tell	told	erzählen
think	thought	denken
wear	wore	tragen
win	won	gewinnen
write	wrote	schreiben

Hier ist eine Liste mit vielen wichtigen unregelmäßigen Verben.

Übung: Irregular verbs

① **Crossword puzzle. Fill in the regular and irregular verbs of the simple past.**

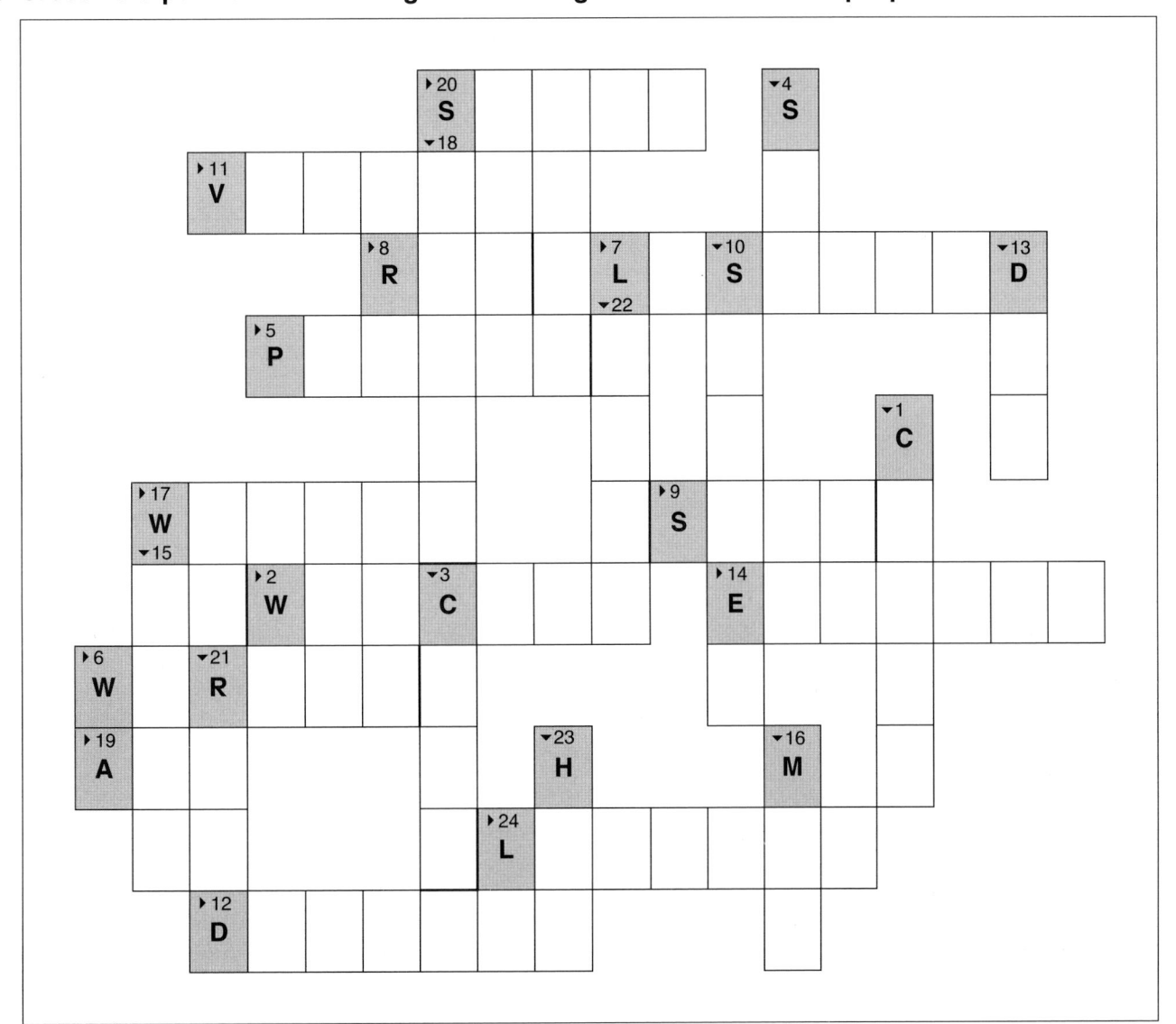

1. aussuchen
2. (TV) schauen
3. kommen
4. sitzen
5. spielen
6. arbeiten
7. zuhören
8. rennen
9. schwimmen
10. zeigen
11. besuchen
12. entscheiden
13. machen, tun
14. genießen
15. schreiben
16. treffen
17. spazieren
18. bleiben
19. essen
20. schlafen
21. lesen
22. leben
23. haben
24. lachen

Übung: Irregular verbs

❶ **Find the 17 regular and irregular verbs of the simple past and mark them (regular verbs green, irregular verbs blue).**

Finde die 17 regelmäßigen und unregelmäßigen Verben im Simple Past in diesem Suchsel und markiere sie mit unterschiedlichen Farben (regelmäßige Verben grün, unregelmäßige Verben blau).

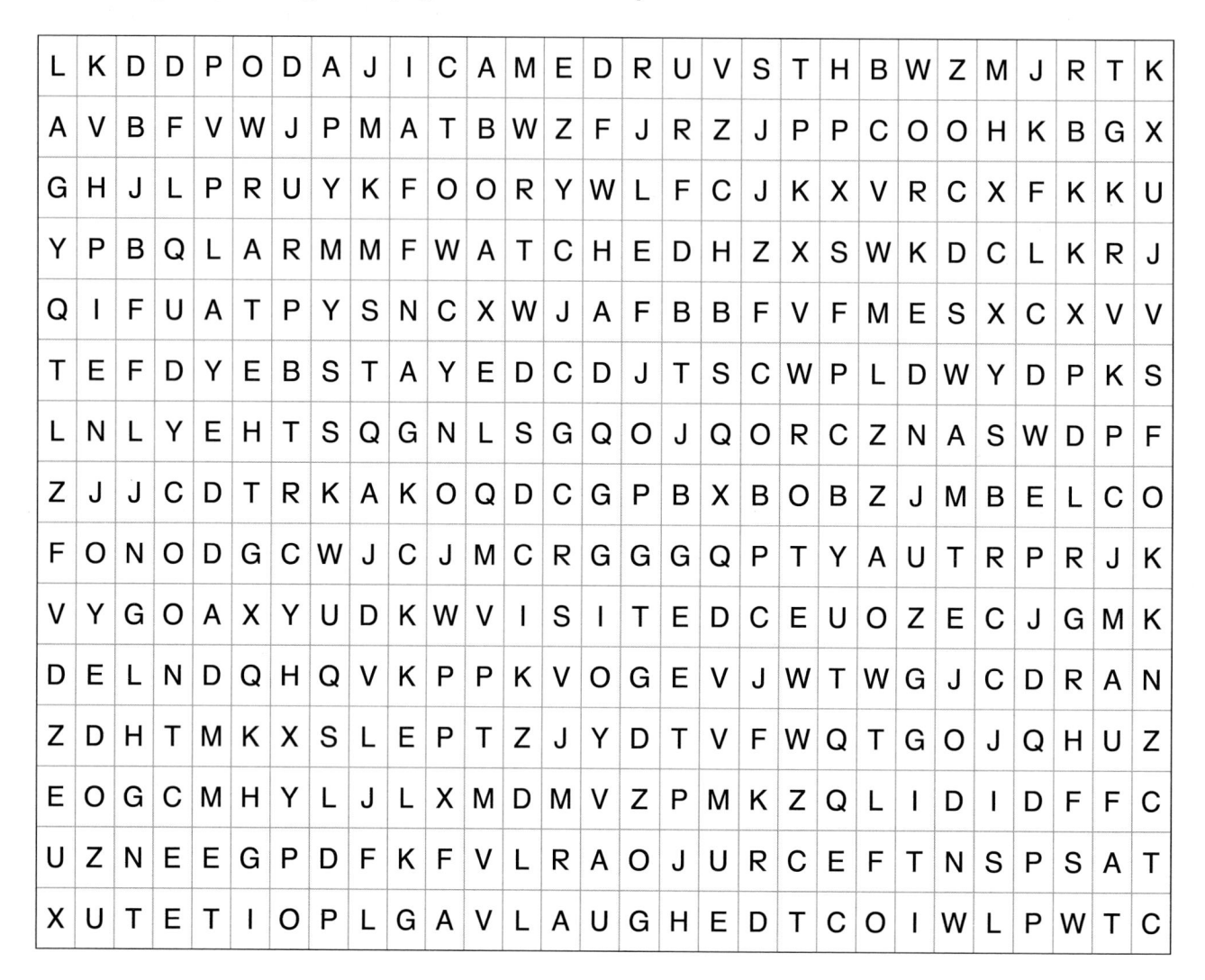

L	K	D	D	P	O	D	A	J	I	C	A	M	E	D	R	U	V	S	T	H	B	W	Z	M	J	R	T	K
A	V	B	F	V	W	J	P	M	A	T	B	W	Z	F	J	R	Z	J	P	P	C	O	O	H	K	B	G	X
G	H	J	L	P	R	U	Y	K	F	O	O	R	Y	W	L	F	C	J	K	X	V	R	C	X	F	K	K	U
Y	P	B	Q	L	A	R	M	M	F	W	A	T	C	H	E	D	H	Z	X	S	W	K	D	C	L	K	R	J
Q	I	F	U	A	T	P	Y	S	N	C	X	W	J	A	F	B	B	F	V	F	M	E	S	X	C	X	V	V
T	E	F	D	Y	E	B	S	T	A	Y	E	D	C	D	J	T	S	C	W	P	L	D	W	Y	D	P	K	S
L	N	L	Y	E	H	T	S	Q	G	N	L	S	G	Q	O	J	Q	O	R	C	Z	N	A	S	W	D	P	F
Z	J	J	C	D	T	R	K	A	K	O	Q	D	C	G	P	B	X	B	O	B	Z	J	M	B	E	L	C	O
F	O	N	O	D	G	C	W	J	C	J	M	C	R	G	G	G	Q	P	T	Y	A	U	T	R	P	R	J	K
V	Y	G	O	A	X	Y	U	D	K	W	V	I	S	I	T	E	D	C	E	U	O	Z	E	C	J	G	M	K
D	E	L	N	D	Q	H	Q	V	K	P	P	K	V	O	G	E	V	J	W	T	W	G	J	C	D	R	A	N
Z	D	H	T	M	K	X	S	L	E	P	T	Z	J	Y	D	T	V	F	W	Q	T	G	O	J	Q	H	U	Z
E	O	G	C	M	H	Y	L	J	L	X	M	D	M	V	Z	P	M	K	Z	Q	L	I	D	I	D	F	F	C
U	Z	N	E	E	G	P	D	F	K	F	V	L	R	A	O	J	U	R	C	E	F	T	N	S	P	S	A	T
X	U	T	E	T	I	O	P	L	G	A	V	L	A	U	G	H	E	D	T	C	O	I	W	L	P	W	T	C

Adjektive

Grammar Box: Adjectives

- Mit Adjektiven kannst du Gegenstände und Personen näher beschreiben.
- Um Gegenstände oder Personen zu vergleichen, benötigst du Steigerungsformen der Adjektive.
- Die erste Steigerungsform der Adjektive (**comparative**) endet auf -er, die zweite Steigerungsform (**superlative**) endet auf -est.
- Adjektive mit zwei oder mehr Silben werden mit *more* (1. Steigerungsform) und *most* (2. Steigerungsform) gesteigert.

Beispiele:

adjective	comparative (1. Steigerungsform)	superlative (2. Steigerungsform)
nice	nic**er**	(the) nic**est**
cool	cool**er**	(the) cool**est**
fast	fast**er**	(the) fast**est**

💡 Beachte folgende Sonderformen:

bad	worse	(the) worst
good	better	(the) best

💡 Bei Adjektiven, die auf -y enden, wird das -y zu -ie und -iest.

funn**y**	funn**ier**	(the) funn**iest**

- Um Gegenstände oder Personen miteinander zu vergleichen, verwendest du die erste Steigerungsform und benutzt für „als" im Englischen *than*.

I am younger **than** you. → Ich bin jünger <u>als</u> du.

My sister is older **than** me. → Meine Schwester ist älter <u>als</u> ich.

💡 Verwechsle *than* („als") nicht mit *then* („dann")!

Sind z. B. die Personen, die du vergleichst, gleich alt, verwendest du „**as** old **as**".

Adjektive: Steigerung und Vergleich (1)

① **Complete the table. Decide which adjective is positive and which one is negative.**

bad · nice · beautiful · cool · aggressive · happy · awful · arrogant

positive	negative

② **Connect the verbs with two or more adjectives and write them down.**

smell	great
feel	beautiful
look	awful
taste	horrible
sound	good

smell: _____

feel: _____

look: _____

taste: _____

sound: _____

Think about examples and write a sentence for each verb.

1. _____

2. _____

3. _____

4. _____

5. _____

Adjektive: Steigerung und Vergleich (2)

③ **Fill in the table with the missing forms.**

adjective	comparative	superlative
	cooler	
		the funniest
good		
		the worst
	more interesting	
beautiful		
	greater	
happy		
		the nicest
	smaller	
big		
strong		

④ **Find the opposites.**

1. short
2. tall
3. easy
4. good
5. sunny

a) bad
b) difficult
c) rainy
d) long
e) small

1	2	3	4	5

Adjektive: Steigerung und Vergleich (3)

5) **What is right and what is wrong? Tick the right box.**

	right	wrong
Sarah is older than Olivia.	☐	☐
Olivia is younger than Tony.	☐	☐
Tony is older than Sarah.	☐	☐
Sarah is younger than Grandma.	☐	☐
Olivia is younger than Sarah.	☐	☐
Tony is as old as Sarah.	☐	☐
Grandma is older than Mum.	☐	☐
Dad is as old as Grandad.	☐	☐

6) **Who is bigger? Who is smaller?**

The butterfly is _____ _____ the cat.

The horse is _____ _____ the mouse.

The mouse is _____ _____ the horse.

The cat is _____ _____ the butterfly.

The horse is _____ _____ the cat.

The cat is _____ _____ the horse.

Adjektive: Steigerung und Vergleich (4)

⑦ **What about you? Compare yourself with friends and write down 3 sentences.**

1. I am older than _____.

2. But I am younger than _____.

3. I am as old as _____.

⑧ **Colder or warmer? Compare the cities and write down sentences.**

London	Paris	Berlin

London is _____ than Paris.
Paris is _____ than London.

Paris is _____ than Berlin.
Berlin is _____ than Paris.

Berlin is _____ than London.
London is _____ than Berlin.

⑨ **Which car is faster – bigger – more expensive? Compare these cars and write down as many sentences as you can.**

_____
_____
_____
_____

Adjektive: Steigerung und Vergleich (5)

⑩ **Which food do you like better, which one is healthier …?**

1. pizza / fish and chips – tasty

   _____

2. salad / sweets – healthy

   _____

3. fast food / chocolate – good

   _____

4. a meal from a restaurant / a meal from a school canteen – expensive

   _____

⑪ **Which food is the best, sweetest …? What do you think?**

1. pizza / fish and chips / spaghetti – good

   → *I think fish and chips is the best of all.*

2. ice cream / cake / biscuits – sweet

   → _____

3. Italian / Indian / Chinese food – spicy

   → _____

4. German cookies / Italian cookies / American cookies – big

   → _____

5. coke / water / juice – healthy

   → _____

6. apples / smartphones / cars – expensive

   → _____

Adjektive: Steigerung und Vergleich (6)

⑫ **Find out and tick the right box!**

adjective	-er / -est	more / most	special form
good	☐	☐	☐
nice	☐	☐	☐
famous	☐	☐	☐
beautiful	☐	☐	☐
cool	☐	☐	☐
bad	☐	☐	☐
expensive	☐	☐	☐
big	☐	☐	☐
tasty	☐	☐	☐
interesting	☐	☐	☐
healthy	☐	☐	☐
strong	☐	☐	☐
warm	☐	☐	☐
easy	☐	☐	☐
cold	☐	☐	☐
difficult	☐	☐	☐
short	☐	☐	☐
happy	☐	☐	☐
exciting	☐	☐	☐

Remember the special forms!

Adjektive: Steigerung und Vergleich (1)

❶ Complete the table. Decide which adjective is positive and which one is negative.

Vervollständige die Tabelle. Welche Adjektive sind negativ und welche positiv?

> bad (*schlecht*) • nice (*nett*) • beautiful (*schön*) • cool • aggressive (*aggressiv*) • happy (*fröhlich*) • awful (*schrecklich*) • arrogant (*hochnäsig*)

positive	negative

❷ Connect the verbs with one or more adjectives and write them down.

Verbinde die Verben mit einem oder mehreren Adjektiven und notiere sie.

smell	great
feel	beautiful
look	awful
taste	horrible
sound	good

smell: _____

feel: _____

look: _____

taste: _____

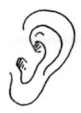

sound: _____

Adjektive: Steigerung und Vergleich (2)

❸ Fill in the table with the missing forms.

Vervollständige die Tabelle.

adjective	comparative	superlative
_ _ _ _	cooler	the _ _ _ _ _ _ _
funny	_ _ _ _ ier	the funniest
good	_ _ tt _ _	the best
bad	_ _ _ _ _	the worst
_ _ _ _ _ _ _ _ _ _ _ _ _	_ _ _ _ interesting	the most interesting
beautiful	_ _ _ _ beautiful	the _ _ _ _ beautiful
great	greater	the great _ _ _
happy	_ _ _ _ ie _	the _ _ _ _ iest
_ _ _ _	nic _ _	the nicest
small	smaller	the _ _ _ _ _ _ _ _ _
big	bigg _ _	the bigg _ _ _
strong	_ _ _ _ _ _ er	the strong _ _ _

❹ Find the opposite.

Finde das Gegenteil.

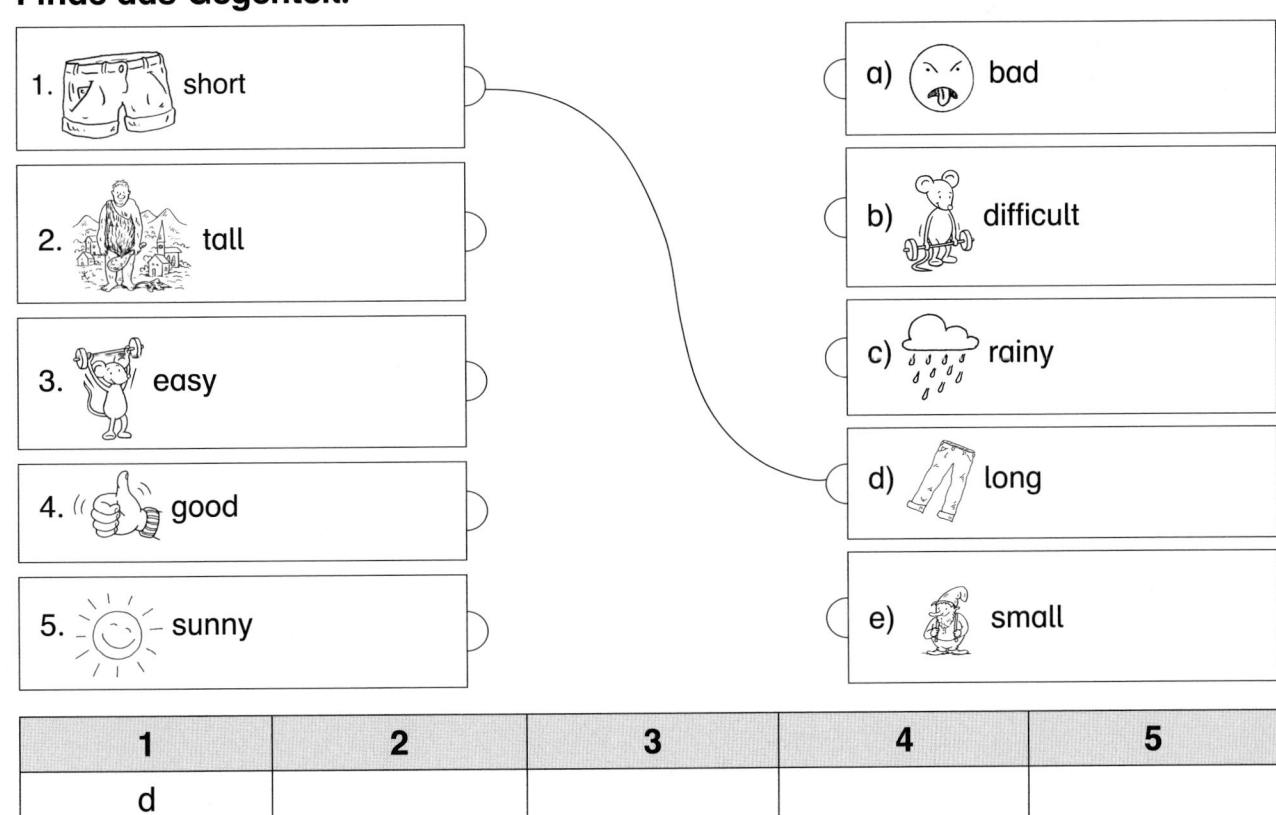

1. short
2. tall
3. easy
4. good
5. sunny

a) bad
b) difficult
c) rainy
d) long
e) small

1	2	3	4	5
d				

Adjektive: Steigerung und Vergleich (3)

❺ **What is right and what is wrong? Tick the correct box.**

Welche Aussagen sind richtig oder welche sind falsch? Kreuze an.

	right	wrong
Sarah is older than Olivia.	☐	☐
Olivia is younger than Tony.	☐	☐
Tony is older than Sarah.	☐	☐
Sarah is younger than Grandma.	☐	☐
Olivia is younger than Sarah.	☐	☐
Tony is as old as Sarah.	☐	☐
Grandma is older than Mum.	☐	☐
Dad is as old as Grandad.	☐	☐

❻ **Who is bigger or smaller?**

Welches Tier ist größer und welches ist kleiner? Beobachte und vergleiche.

The butterfly is _____ _____ the cat.

The horse is _____ _____ the mouse.

The mouse is _____ _____ the horse.

The cat is _____ _____ the butterfly.

The horse is _____ _____ the cat.

The cat is _____ _____ the horse.

Adjektive: Steigerung und Vergleich (4)

❼ What about you? Compare yourself with friends and write down 3 sentences.
Vergleiche dich mit deinen Freunden und schreibe 3 Sätze auf.

1. I am older than _____. *(älter als)*

2. But I am younger than _____. *(jünger als)*

3. I am as old as _____. *(so alt wie)*

❽ Colder or warmer? Compare the cities and write down sentences.
Kälter oder wärmer? Vergleiche die Städte und vervollständige die Sätze.

cold ⟶ colder
warm ⟶ warmer

London	Paris	Berlin

London is _____ than Paris.

Paris is _____ than London.

Paris is _____ than Berlin.

Berlin is _____ than Paris.

Berlin is _____ than London.

London is _____ than Berlin.

Adjektive: Steigerung und Vergleich (5)

❾ Which car is faster – bigger – more expensive? Compare these cars and write down as many sentences as you can.

Welches Auto ist schneller, größer oder teurer? Vergleiche die Autos und schreibe so viele Vergleichssätze wie möglich auf.

big	bigger	as big as
fast	faster	as fast as
expensive	more expensive	as expensive as

car   ambulance   racing car

Adjektive: Steigerung und Vergleich (6)

❿ Which food do you like better, which is healthier …?
Welches Essen magst du lieber, welches ist gesünder …? Bilde Sätze.

1. pizza / fish and chips – tastier

   _____

2. salad / sweets – healthier

   _____

3. fast food / chocolate – better

   _____

4. a meal from a restaurant / a meal from a school canteen – more expensive

   _____

⓫ Which food is the best, sweetest …? What do you think?
Was schmeckt am besten, süßesten …? Was meinst du?

1. pizza / fish and chips / spaghetti – the best

   → _I think fish and chips is the best of all._

2. ice cream / cake / biscuits – the sweetest

   → _____

3. Italian / Indian / Chinese food – the spiciest

   → _____

4. German cookies / Italian cookies / American cookies – the biggest

   → _____

5. coke / water / juice – the healthiest

   → _____

6. apples / smartphones / cars – the most expensive

   → _____

Adjektive: Steigerung und Vergleich (7)

① Find out and tick the right box. Remember the special forms!

adjective	-er / -est	more / most	special form
good	☐	☐	☐
nice	☐	☐	☐
famous	☐	☐	☐
beautiful	☐	☐	☐
cool	☐	☐	☐
bad	☐	☐	☐
expensive	☐	☐	☐
bi**g**	☐	☐	☐
tast**y**	☐	☐	☐
interesting	☐	☐	☐
health**y**	☐	☐	☐
strong	☐	☐	☐
warm	☐	☐	☐
eas**y**	☐	☐	☐
cold	☐	☐	☐
difficult	☐	☐	☐
short	☐	☐	☐
ha**pp**y	☐	☐	☐
exciting	☐	☐	☐

Setze den Haken in das richtige Feld. Achte besonders auf die dick gedruckten Wörter und Buchstaben!

Adverbien

Grammar Box: Adverbs

Adverbien beziehen sich auf das Verb (lat. *ad* = „zu" / *verbum* = „Verb"). Sie beschreiben die Tätigkeit bzw. wie du etwas machst (gut kochen, schnell laufen …).

Adverbien stehen meist am Satzende. Angaben zu Ort und Zeit stehen nach dem Adverb.

Du bildest die Adverbien, indem du an das Adjektiv ein *-ly* anhängst.

Beispiel:

quick → quickly

He is a quick runner. Er ist ein schneller Läufer.

→ Bezug zum Nomen (Was für ein Läufer ist er? – Ein schneller Läufer.)

He runs quickly. Er läuft schnell.

→ Bezug auf die Tätigkeit (Wie läuft er? – Schnell.)

Beachte folgende Schreibweisen und Sonderformen:
angry – angrily / easy – easily
fast – fast
good – well
hard – hard

Adverbien: Übungen (1)

① **Find the adjectives (green) and adverbes (blue) and colour them.**

bad   strong   beautifully   quickly   carefully   well
angry   terrible   happy   fast
NERVOUSLY   good   easily   quick

② **Complete the sentences with adverbs.**

1. The girl is looking _____ at her dog. (happy)

2. The team played _____. (good)

3. When you write the postcard for your grandparents please write _____. (clear)

4. I worked _____ for the test, but I still failed. (hard)

5. I watched a thriller last night. That's why I didn't sleep _____. (good)

6. It is raining _____ (heavy), so we can't go outside.

7. You have to check the task _____. (careful)

8. You can earn money _____ (easy) with babysitting.

9. The cat moved _____ (quick) when we came in.

10. The dog barked _____. (loud)

11. He shouldn't take part in this competition because he sings _____. (terrible)

12. Children learn to ride their bikes _____. (easy)

13. When we arrived our friends waved _____. (happy)

14. It was his first date. He waited for the girl _____. (nervous)

Adverbien: Übungen (2)

③ How do you do the things? Fill in suitable (*passende*) adverbs.

1. I clean my room _____.

2. I brush my teeth _____.

3. I do my homework _____.

4. I practise for the tests _____.

5. I ride my bike _____.

6. I run very _____.

④ Adjective or adverb? Write two sentences – use the adjective and the adverb once.

funny – funnily • clear – clearly • beautiful – beautifully • happy – happily • careful – carefully

1. *This is a funny boy.*

   He tells stories funnily.

2. _____

   _____

3. _____

   _____

4. _____

   _____

5. _____

   _____

Adverbien: Übungen (1)

❶ Find the adjectives (green) and adverbes (blue) and colour them.

Finde die Adjektive (grün) und Adverbien (blau) und kreise sie farbig ein.

---

angry • terrible • happy • fast • beautifully • bad • strong

quickly • carefully • well • easily • quick

nervously • good

---

❷ Complete the sentences with adverbs.

Vervollständige die Sätze mit Adverbien.

1. The girl is looking _____ at her dog. (happy – happily)

2. The team played _____. (good – well)

3. When you write the postcard for your grandparents please write _____. (clear – clearly)

4. I worked _____ for the test, but I still failed. (hard – hard)

5. I watched a thriller last night. That's why I didn't sleep _____. (good – well)

6. It is raining _____, so we can't go outside. (heavy – heavily)

7. You have to check the task _____. (careful – carefully)

8. You can earn money _____ with babysitting. (easy – easily)

9. The cat moved _____ when we came in. (quick – quickly)

10. The dog barked _____. (loud – loudly)

11. He shouldn't take part in this competition because he sings _____. (terrible – terribly)

12. Children learn to ride their bikes _____. (easy – easily)

13. When we arrived our friends waved _____. (happy – happily)

14. It was his first date. He waited for the girl _____. (nervous – nervously)

Adverbien: Übungen (2)

❸ How do you do the things? Fill in suitable adverbs.

Wie erledigst du die Dinge? Finde passende Adverbien aus der Box.

> fast (2x) • quickly • regularly • carefully • perfectly

1. I clean my room _____.

2. I brush my teeth _____.

3. I do my homework _____.

4. I practise for the tests _____.

5. I ride my bike _____.

6. I run very _____.

❹ Adjective or adverb? Write two sentences – use the adjective and the adverb once.

Adjektiv oder Adverb? Schreibe zwei Sätze. Verwende jeweils ein Adjektiv und ein Adverb.

> funny – funnily • clear – clearly • beautiful – beautifully • happy – happily • careful – carefully

1. *This is a funny girl.*

   She tells stories funnily.

2. _____

3. _____

4. _____

5. _____

Possessivpronomen

Grammar Box: Possessive Pronouns

Possessivbegleiter zeigen an, wem etwas gehört oder zu wem jemand gehört.

Im Englischen:

personal pronouns	possessive adjectives	possessive pronouns
I	my	**mine**
you	your	**yours**
he	his	**his**
she	her	**hers**
it	its	**its**
we	our	**ours**
you	your	**yours**
they	their	**theirs**

- Possessivbegleiter: *my, your* (im Singular und Plural), *his, her, its, our, their*
- Possessivpronomen: *mine, yours* (im Singular und Plural), *his, hers, its, ours, theirs*

Im Deutschen:

Personalpronomen	Possessivbegleiter	Possessivpronomen
ich	mein	meins
du	dein	deins
er	sein	seins
sie	ihr	ihres
es	sein	seins
wir	unser	unseres
ihr	euer	eures
sie	ihr	ihres

Merke dir:
This is **my book**. Dies ist **mein Buch**.
This book is **mine**. Dieses Buch ist **meins**.

It's not **your book**. Es ist nicht **dein Buch**.
It's not **yours**. Es ist nicht **deins**.

Possessivpronomen: Übungen (1)

① **Find the pronouns and fill in the table.**

L	K	D	D	P	O	D	A	J	I	C	A	Z	E	Y	R	F	O	B	A	M	Q
A	V	B	F	V	W	J	P	M	A	T	B	W	Z	S	J	O	P	I	T	J	S
G	H	J	L	P	E	U	Y	K	F	O	I	R	Y	E	L	F	R	L	Y	U	C
Y	I	B	Q	L	A	R	M	M	F	H	T	K	E	T	P	D	G	M	H	N	V
Q	S	F	U	A	T	P	Y	I	T	C	S	H	E	A	F	B	V	H	E	H	B
T	E	F	D	O	E	B	S	N	H	Y	E	D	C	Y	J	T	E	T	C	Z	N
H	N	L	Y	U	H	T	S	E	E	N	L	S	G	O	A	J	D	R	E	B	O
E	J	J	C	R	T	R	K	A	I	O	Q	D	C	U	P	B	V	F	F	T	Z
Y	O	N	O	S	G	C	W	J	R	J	H	X	N	D	G	M	Q	S	V	G	R
V	N	O	Q	G	C	Y	U	D	S	W	V	K	S	O	T	E	S	W	T	R	E
T	N	L	Y	N	H	Q	U	E	M	N	L	S	G	U	A	J	Y	Y	H	F	W
P	J	Z	C	P	T	R	K	A	P	A	K	D	C	M	H	B	X	X	W	V	P
Y	O	U	R	S	B	F	W	J	R	Z	B	H	E	R	S	T	U	B	D	C	U
V	H	Q	L	U	C	Y	U	D	S	C	R	T	V	Z	J	M	J	T	Q	S	D

I	mine

② **Which one is wrong?**

1. I – ~~you~~ – mine
2. hers – she – ours
3. we – theirs – ours
4. they – his – theirs
5. his – he – yours
6. you – he – yours
7. its – theirs – it
8. you – yours – mine

Possessivpronomen: Übungen (2)

③ **Whose book is it? Complete the sentences with the possessive adjectives and pronouns.**

> my (3x) • your (4x) • yours (3x) • mine (2x) • her (2x) • our

Olivia: I am looking for _____ book. Can you help me, please?

Ben: Did you check _____ bag?

Olivia: Yes, I have already checked _____ bag, but it's not there.

Ben: Hm, okay, let's look in _____ classroom.

Maybe it's on _____ desk.

Olivia: Look, I found it.

Ben: Oh no, Olivia. I'm sorry, but that's not _____. It's _____. But look over there.

The blue one. It could be _____.

Olivia: No, that's Sarah's book. _____ book has _____ name on the cover, you see?

I don't want to look for the book anymore. Please let's say that _____ is _____.

Ben: But Olivia, you know, Mrs Mitchell will be angry if you don't find _____ book.

Olivia: Oh look! There is _____ book under the desk.

Ben: That's great. You found _____ book.

④ **Check your partner's pens, books, bags … and write down.**

My pen is blue and yours is red. *My bag is …*

1. _____
2. _____
3. _____
4. _____

Possessivpronomen: Übungen (1)

❶ Find the pronouns and fill in the table.

Finde die Pronomen und fülle die Tabelle aus.

L	K	D	D	Y	O	U	A	J	I	C	A	Z	E	Y	R	U
A	V	B	F	V	W	J	P	M	A	Y	B	W	Z	H	J	R
G	H	J	L	P	E	U	Y	K	F	O	I	R	Y	E	L	F
Y	I	T	Q	L	A	R	M	M	F	U	T	K	E	T	P	D
Q	S	F	U	A	T	P	Y	I	T	C	S	H	E	A	F	B
T	E	F	D	O	E	B	S	N	H	Y	E	D	C	Y	J	T
H	N	L	Y	U	H	T	S	E	E	N	L	S	G	O	A	J
E	J	J	C	R	T	R	K	A	I	O	Q	D	C	U	P	B
Y	O	N	O	S	G	C	W	J	R	J	H	E	R	S	G	M
V	Y	O	U	R	S	Y	U	D	S	W	V	K	S	O	T	E

I	mine

I	mine

❷ Which one is wrong? Cross it out.

Welches Wort der Reihe ist falsch? Streiche durch.

1. I – ~~you~~ – mine
2. hers – she – ours
3. we – theirs – ours
4. they – his – theirs
5. his – he – yours
6. you – he – yours
7. its – theirs – it
8. you – yours – mine

Possessivpronomen: Übungen (2)

❸ Whose book is it? Complete the sentences with the possessive adjectives and pronouns.

Wessen Buch ist das? Vervollständige die Sätze mit den richtigen Possessivbegleitern und Possessivpronomen.

> my (3x) • your (4x) • yours (3x) • mine (2x) • her • our • Her

Olivia: I am looking for _____ (mein) book. Can you help me, please?

Ben: Did you check _____ (deine) bag?

Olivia: Yes, I have already checked _____ (meine) bag, but it's not there.

Ben: Hm, okay, let's look in _____ (unserem) classroom. Maybe it's on _____ (deinem) desk.

Olivia: Look, I found it.

Ben: Oh no, Olivia. I'm sorry, but that's not _____ (deins). It's _____ (meins). But look over there. The blue one. It could be _____ (deins).

Olivia: No, that's Sarah's book. _____ (Ihr) book has _____ (ihren) name on the cover, you see? I don't want to look for the book anymore. Please let's say that _____ (deins) is _____ (meins).

Ben: But Olivia, you know, Mrs Mitchell will be angry if you don't find _____ (dein) book.

Olivia: Oh look! There is _____ (mein) book under the desk.

Ben: That's great. You found _____ (dein) book.

❹ Check your partner's pens, books, bags … and write down.

Schaue in die Schultasche deines Nachbarn und schreibe auf.

<u>My pen is blue and yours is red.</u> *My bag is …*

My _____ and yours is _____ .

My _____ and yours is _____ .

My _____ and yours is _____ .

My _____ and yours is _____ .

Mengenangaben

Grammar Box: some and any / much and many

some and any

- Die Begriffe *some* und *any* verwendest du, um eine unbestimmte Menge auszudrücken.
- Das Wort *some* verwendest du in bejahten Aussagen und höflichen Fragen.
- Das Wort *any* verwendest du in Fragen und verneinten Sätzen.
- Die Begriffe *some* und *any* kannst du mit „ein paar", „etwas" übersetzen.

Beispiele:

I'm looking for some books. (bejaht)
Would you like some biscuits? (Angebot) → *some*
Can I have some biscuits, please? (höfliche Frage)

I haven't got any books. (verneint) → *any*
Have you got any books? (Frage)

much and many

- Die Begriffe *much* und *many* verwendest du, um eine bestimmte Menge auszudrücken.
- Das Wort *many* verwendest du bei **zählbaren** Gegenständen/Personen im Plural („viele").
- Das Wort *much* verwendest du bei **nicht zählbaren** Gegenständen („viel").
- Das Wort *much* bedeutet „viel" und *many* bedeutet „viele".

How many apples do we have? – **Wie viele** Äpfel haben wir?
Not **many**. – Nicht **viele**.

Hoch much money do we have? – Wie viel Geld haben wir?
Not **much**. – Nicht **viel**.

Mengenangaben: some and any (1)

① **What's in the fridge? Fill in *some* or *any*.**

1. There are _____ eggs, but there aren't _____ apples.

2. There are _____ sausages, but there isn't _____ juice.

3. There is _____ cheese, but there aren't _____ sweets.

4. There is _____ milk, but there isn't _____ chocolate.

② **The shopping list**

Lucy and her brother Ben have to do the shopping. They are looking at their list. Complete the sentences.

Lucy: We have to buy _____ coffee.

Ben: We don't have to buy _____ coke.

Lucy: We have to buy _____ potatoes.

Ben: We don't have to buy _____ tomatoes.

Lucy: We have to buy _____ bread.

Ben: We don't have to buy _____ cake.

Lucy: We have to buy _____ bananas.

Ben: We don't have to buy _____ apples.

- coffee
- ~~coke~~
- potatoes
- ~~tomatoes~~
- bread
- ~~cake~~
- bananas
- ~~apples~~

5 Mengenangaben: some and any (2)

③ **What's in your bag?**

Have a look and write down what's in your bag and what's not in your bag. Start like this:

In my bag there are some sweets.

④ **Shopping list for the party**

You are in the supermarket and you want to buy some things for your birthday party tonight. Write down what you need to buy and what you don't need to buy.

I need to buy some coke, but I don't need to buy any water.

Mengenangaben: some and any (1)

❶ What's in the fridge? Fill in *some* or *any*.

Was ist im Kühlschrank? Setze *some* oder *any* ein.

1. **There are** <u>some</u> eggs,

    but **there aren't** <u>any</u> apples.

2. **There are** _____ sausages,

    but **there isn't** _____ juice.

3. **There is** _____ cheese,

    but **there aren't** _____ sweets.

4. **There is** _____ milk,

    but **there isn't** _____ chocolate.

❷ The shopping list

Lucy and her brother Ben have to do the shopping. They are looking at their list. Complete the sentences.

Lucy und ihr Bruder Ben müssen einkaufen. Sie schauen auf ihre Liste. Vervollständige die Sätze.

> 💡 **Denk daran: + some / – any**

Lucy: **We have** to buy <u>some</u> coffee.

Ben: **We don't have** to buy <u>any</u> coke.

Lucy: We have to buy _____ potatoes.

Ben: We don't have to buy _____ tomatoes.

Lucy: We have to buy _____ bread.

Ben: We don't have to buy _____ cake.

Lucy: We have to buy _____ bananas.

Ben: We don't have to buy _____ apples.

Shopping list:
- coffee
- potatoes
- bread
- bananas
- ~~coke~~
- ~~tomatoes~~
- ~~cake~~
- ~~apples~~

Mengenangaben: some and any (2)

③ What's in your bag?

Have a look and write down what's in your bag (*some*) and what's not in your bag (*any*).

Was ist in deiner Schultasche?

Schau hinein und notiere, was sich darin befindet (*some*) und was sich nicht darin befindet (*any*).

In my bag …

there is / are **some**	there isn't / aren't **any**
some sandwiches	

④ Your shopping list for the party

You are in the supermarket and you want to buy some things for your birthday party tonight. Write down what you buy and what not.

Du bist im Supermarkt und feierst heute Abend eine Party. Schreibe auf, was du kaufst und was nicht.

Example: I buy some coke, but I don't buy any water.

I buy some coke,	but I don't buy any water.
I buy some …	but …
I buy some …	but …

Mengenangaben: much and many (1)

① **Which nouns are countable (*zählbar*) and which ones are uncountable (*unzählbar*)? Fill in the table.**

tea • streets • books • comics • time • biscuits • coffee • bottles • help • flour

zählbar / many	unzählbar / much

② **Fill the blanks with *much* or *many*.**

1. Are there _____ hotels in London?

2. My sister loves reading. She has _____ books in her room.

3. If you want to become famous one day, you should know _____ people.

4. We still have _____ time, so we don't need to hurry up.

5. My father travels a lot. He has seen _____ countries.

6. That's a big project. We need _____ help.

7. We need _____ food for the party. There are _____ guests.

8. Even if they don't eat _____, I want to have _____ plates.

9. It's the end of the month and I don't have _____ money.

10. We didn't have _____ petrol, so our car stopped on the highway.

11. We need to stay in your house because there aren't _____ hotels near the city.

Mengenangaben: much and many (2)

③ **How much or how many? Fill in the blanks.**

_____ _____ money did you pay for your new bike?

_____ _____ students failed this exam?

_____ _____ weeks did you stay in the hotel?

_____ _____ juice did buy for the party?

_____ _____ cakes did your mother prepare?

_____ _____ members does this club have?

④ **Circle the right word.**

My mother drinks much / many coffee.

I have much / many money.

My brother watches much / many TV series.

Olivia spends much / many time at school.

There was much / many traffic.

We had much / many fun at the party.

There were much / many accidents on the road.

There are much / many interesting things in a museum.

Mengenangaben: much and many (1)

❶ Which nouns are countable and which ones are uncountable? Fill in the table.
Welche Nomen sind zählbar, welche unzählbar? Trage in die Tabelle ein.

tea • streets • books • comics • time • biscuits • coffee • bottles • help • flour (*Mehl*)

zählbar / many	unzählbar / much

❷ Fill in the blanks with *much* or *many*. Look at the nouns. Are they countable or uncountable?

Setze *much* oder *many* ein. Achte dabei auf die fett gedruckten Nomen! Überlege, ob diese Dinge zählbar (*many*) oder nicht zählbar (*much*) sind.

1. Are there _____ **hotels** in London?

2. My sister loves reading. She has _____ **books** in her room.

3. If you want to become famous one day, you should know _____ **people**.

4. We still have _____ **time**, so we don't need to hurry up.

5. My father travels a lot. He has seen _____ **countries**.

6. That's a big project. We need _____ **help**.

7. We need _____ **food** for the party. There are _____ **guests**.

8. Even if they don't eat _____ , I want to have _____ **plates**.

9. It's the end of the month and I don't have _____ **money**.

10. We didn't have _____ **petrol**, so our car stopped on the highway.

11. We need to stay in your house because there aren't _____ **hotels** near the city.

> Denk daran: *many* bei zählbaren und *much* bei nicht zählbaren Gegenständen und Dingen!

Mengenangaben: much and many (2)

③ How much or how many? Fill in *how much* or *how many*.
Setze *how much* („wie viel") oder *how many* („wie viele") ein.

1. _____ _____ **money** did you pay for your new bike?
2. _____ _____ **students** failed this exam?
3. _____ _____ **weeks** did you stay in the hotel?
4. _____ _____ **juice** did buy for the party?
5. _____ _____ **cakes** did your mother prepare?
6. _____ _____ **members** (*Mitglieder*) does this club have?

④ Circle the right word. The bold nouns will help you.
Kreise das richtige Wort ein. Achte auf die dick gedruckten Wörter.

1. My mother drinks much / many **coffee**.

2. I have much / many **money**.

3. My brother watches much / many **TV series**.

4. Olivia spends much / many **time** at school.

5. There was much / many **traffic**.

6. We had much / many **fun** at the party.

7. There were much / many **accidents** on the road.

8. There are much / many **interesting things** in a museum.

6 Present Perfect

Grammar Box: Present Perfect

Mit dem Present Perfect lernst du eine weitere Zeitform der Vergangenheit. Du verwendest es, um auszudrücken, dass etwas passiert ist und eine Auswirkung auf die Gegenwart hat. Du verwendest es auch, um auszudrücken, dass eine Handlung gerade erst abgeschlossen wurde.

- <u>Bildung</u>: Das Present Perfect wird gebildet aus *have / has* + past participle (3. Form)

  💡 Merke: Bei *he / she / it* verwendest du *has*!

Beachte, dass die regelmäßigen Formen des Past Participle auf *-ed* enden. Die unregelmäßigen Verben musst du auswendig lernen.

Regular verbs

infinitive	simple past (2. Form)	past participle (3. Form)
play	played	played
watch	watched	watched

Irregular verbs

see	saw	seen
buy	bought	bought

- <u>Beispiele</u>:

Dad has bought this car a long time ago. – He is still driving it.
Papa hat dieses Auto vor langer Zeit gekauft. – Er fährt es immer noch.

Do you want to eat something? – No, thanks, I have just eaten a sandwich.
Möchtest du etwas essen? – Nein, danke. Ich hatte gerade ein Sandwich.

- <u>Verneinung</u>: *have* + *not* + past participle (3. Form)

I haven't eaten lunch **yet**. – Ich habe noch nicht zu Mittag gegessen.

Signal words: *already* („bereits") steht bei Aussagen, *ever* („jemals") und *yet* („noch nicht") stehen bei Fragen und Verneinungen:

I have **already** done my homework. – Ich habe meine Hausaufgaben bereits gemacht.

Have you **ever** been to England? – Bist du jemals in England gewesen?

She hasn't done her homework **yet**. – Sie hat ihre Hausaufgaben noch nicht gemacht.

Present Perfect

IRREGULAR VERBS

infinitive	simple past	past participle	German
be	was, were	been	sein
become	became	become	werden
break	broke	broken	brechen
buy	bought	bought	kaufen
choose	chose	chosen	aussuchen, wählen
come	came	come	kommen
do	did	done	machen, tun
eat	ate	eaten	essen
fall	fell	fallen	fallen, hinfallen
feed	fed	fed	füttern
feel	felt	felt	fühlen
find	found	found	finden
forget	forgot	forgotten	vergessen
get	got	got	bekommen
give	gave	given	geben
go	went	gone	gehen
have	had	had	haben
hear	heard	heard	hören
know	knew	known	wissen
make	made	made	machen, tun
meet	met	met	treffen
put	put	put	stellen, legen, setzen
read	read	read	lesen
run	ran	run	laufen
say	said	said	sagen
see	saw	seen	sehen
send	sent	sent	verschicken, versenden
sing	sang	sung	singen
sit	sat	sat	sitzen
sleep	slept	slept	schlafen
take	took	taken	nehmen
teach	taught	taught	unterrichten, lehren
tell	told	told	erzählen
think	thought	thought	denken
wear	wore	worn	tragen
win	won	won	gewinnen
write	wrote	written	schreiben

Hier ist eine Liste mit vielen wichtigen unregelmäßigen Verben.

Present Perfect: Aussagen (1)

① **Get used to the third form and fill in the table.**

infinitive	simple past	past participle	German
be	was, were		sein
become	became		werden
buy	bought		kaufen
choose	chose		aussuchen, wählen
come	came		kommen
do	did		machen, tun
eat	ate		essen
fall	fell		fallen, hinfallen
feed	fed		füttern
find	found		finden
get	got		bekommen
give	gave		geben
go	went		gehen
have	had		haben
know	knew		wissen
make	made		machen, tun
meet	met		treffen
put	put		stellen, legen, setzen
run	ran		laufen
say	said		sagen
see	saw		sehen
sing	sang		singen
sit	sat		sitzen
sleep	slept		schlafen
take	took		nehmen
tell	told		erzählen
think	thought		denken
wear	wore		tragen
write	wrote		schreiben

Present Perfect: Aussagen (2)

② **What has Luke done?**

1. *He has tidied up his room.*

2. _____

3. _____

4. _____

5. _____

6. _____

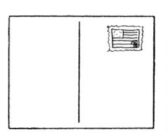

③ **Complete the sentences with a verb from the box. Use the present perfect.**

buy • finish • invite • take • read • forget (2x)

1. I _____ that book. I don't need it anymore. You can take it.

2. Olivia _____ her key outside. She can't find it anymore.

3. My mum _____ new shoes. They are really nice.

4. It's my birthday tomorrow and I _____ all my friends.

5. I _____ the dog for a walk. Now it's your turn.

6. My father _____ his project, that's why he is happy now.

7. I know that girl, but I _____ her name.

Present Perfect: Aussagen (3)

④ **What has happened? Use these verbs to describe it.**

forget • win • climb • break • miss

_____

_____

_____

_____

_____

⑤ **What have they already done? Complete the sentences and use *already*.**

my sister	do	homework
Dad	prepare	mouse
Mum	catch	sandwiches
I	drink	coffee
my brother	repair	bike
my friend	go for a walk	dog

Present Perfect: Aussagen (1)

❶ Get used to the third form and fill in the table. The gaps will help you.
Vervollständige die Tabelle mit der 3. Form. Die Linien helfen dir.

infinitive	simple past	past participle	German
be	was, were	_ _ _ _	sein
become	became	_ _ _ _ _ _	werden
break	broke	_ _ _ _ _	brechen
buy	bought	_ _ _ _ _ _	kaufen
choose	chose	_ _ _ _ _	aussuchen, wählen
come	came	_ _ _ _	kommen
do	did	_ _ _	machen, tun
eat	ate	_ _ _ _ _	essen
fall	fell	_ _ _ _ _ _	fallen, hinfallen
feed	fed	_ _ _	füttern
find	found	_ _ _ _ _	finden
get	got	_ _ _	bekommen
give	gave	_ _ _ _	geben
go	went	_ _ _ _	gehen
have	had	_ _ _	haben
hear	heard	_ _ _ _	hören
know	knew	_ _ _ _ _	wissen
make	made	_ _ _ _	machen, tun
meet	met	_ _ _	treffen
put	put	_ _ _	stellen, legen, setzen
run	ran	_ _ _	laufen
say	said	_ _ _ _	sagen
see	saw	_ _ _ _	sehen
sing	sang	_ _ _ _	singen
sit	sat	_ _ _	sitzen
sleep	slept	_ _ _ _ _	schlafen
take	took	_ _ _ _ _	nehmen
tell	told	_ _ _ _	erzählen
think	thought	_ _ _ _ _ _ _	denken

Present Perfect: Aussagen (2)

❷ What has Luke done? Combine the sentences with the right pictures.
Was hat Luke bereits alles erledigt? Ordne die Sätze den Bildern zu.

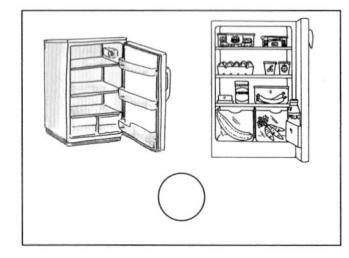

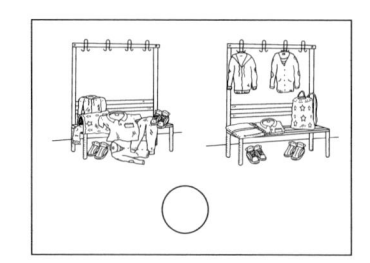

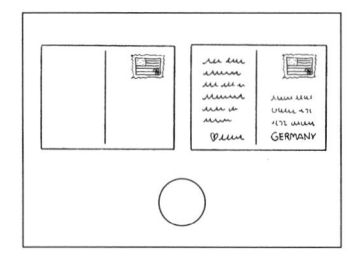

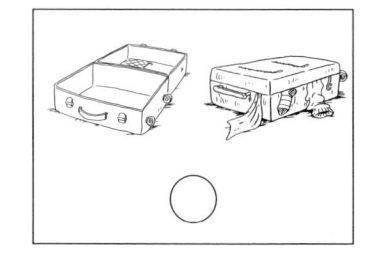

1. He has tidied up his room.
2. He has packed his suitcase.
3. He has washed the dishes.
4. He has written a postcard.
5. He has filled the fridge.
6. He has taken a shower.

❸ Complete the sentences. Use the present perfect.
Vervollständige die Sätze. Verwende das Present Perfect.

1. I _____ _____ (read) that book. I don't need it anymore. You can take it.
2. Olivia _____ _____ (forget) her key outside. She can't find it anymore.
3. My mum _____ _____ (buy) new shoes. They are really nice.
4. It's my birthday tomorrow and I _____ _____ (invite) all my friends.
5. I _____ _____ (take) the dog for a walk. Now it's your turn.
6. My father _____ _____ (finish) his project, that's why he is happy now.
7. I know that girl, but I _____ _____ (forget) her name.

Present Perfect: Aussagen (3)

4 What has happened? Match the sentences and the pictures.

Was ist passiert? Verbinde die Sätze mit den Bildern.

- We have climbed the mountain.
- I have won the race.
- I have forgotten my exercise books.
- I have dropped the cup.
- I have missed the bus.

5 What have they already done? Complete the sentences and use *already*.

Was haben die Personen bereits gemacht? Vervollständige die Sätze. Verwende dabei das Signalwort *already* („bereits").

~~my sister~~ Dad Mum I my brother	have/has	already	~~done~~ prepared cleaned made drunk	~~the homework.~~ a cake. the kitchen. sandwiches. a coffee.

1. *My sister has already done the homework.*

2. _____

3. _____

4. _____

5. _____

Present Perfect: Verneinung

① **It's party time. What have they done?**

✔ buy coke	✔ take out CDs
✘ buy water	✘ take out music box
✔ decorate room	✔ make a cake
✘ decorate garden	✘ make sandwiches

The friends have already _____.

But they haven't _____.

The friends have already _____.

But they haven't _____.

The friends have already _____.

But they haven't _____.

The friends have already _____.

But they haven't _____.

② **You haven't done everything! Choose 5 of these places/things and write down what you have never visited or have never done.**

visit Disneyland • play rugby • watch a thriller • take a taxi home • spend 200 € for a jacket • win the lottery • take part in a circus • ~~visit New York~~ • do bungee jumping

Example: I have never visited New York.

1. _____

2. _____

3. _____

4. _____

5. _____

Present Perfect: Verneinung

❶ It's party time. What have they done?

Es ist Party-Zeit. Was haben sie alles schon erledigt?

- ✔ have bought coke
- ✘ have bought water
- ✔ have decorated room
- ✘ have decorated garden
- ✔ have taken out CDs
- ✘ have taken out music box
- ✔ have made a cake
- ✘ have made sandwiches

The friends have already …	But they haven't …
bought coke.	bought water.

❷ You haven't done everything! Choose 5 of these places/things and write down what you have never visited or done.

Wähle 5 Orte oder Dinge aus, die du noch nicht besucht oder gemacht hast.

> have … visited Disneyland • played rugby • watched a thriller • taken a taxi home • spent 200 € for a jacket • won the lottery • taken part in a circus • ~~visited New York~~ • done bungee jumping

Example: I have <u>never</u> visited New York.

1. _____
2. _____
3. _____
4. _____
5. _____

Present Perfect: Fragen

① **Have you ever …? Write down six questions and ask your friend.**

Example: Have you ever visited Paris? – Yes, I have visited Paris. / No, I haven't visited Paris.

② **What have you done in your life? Think about special or crazy things and write them down.**

Example: I have met Prince Harry.

Present Perfect: Fragen

❶ Have you ever ...?

Write down three questions and ask your friend.

Hast du jemals ...?

Schreibe drei Fragen auf und stelle sie anschließend deinem Partner oder deiner Partnerin.

Example: *Have you ever visited Paris? –*
Yes, I have visited Paris. / No, I haven't visited Paris.

Have you ever _____?

_____.

_____?

_____.

_____?

_____.

❷ What have you done in your life? Think about special or crazy things and write them down.

Überlege, was du bisher an besonderen oder verrückten Dingen gemacht hast, und schreibe sie auf.

Example: *I have met Prince Harry.*

I have ...

_____

_____

_____

Going-to-Future

Grammar Box: Going-to-Future

Das Going-to-Future verwendest du, um zu sagen, was du vorhast.
Dabei geht es um feste Pläne oder Absichten.

Bildung: Du bildest das Going-to-Future mit einer Form von *to be* + *going to* + Verb.
Die Form von *to be* kannst du natürlich auch in der Kurzform nutzen.

long form	short form
I am going to	I'm going to
you are going to	you're going to
he/she/it is going to	he's/she's/it's going to
we are going to	we're going to
you are going to	you're going to
they are going to	they're going to

Beispiele:

My father bought tickets for the match. We are going to watch it on Saturday.

We are going to have a party this weekend.

Verneinung:

I am not going to … / I'm not going to …

Fragen:

There's your favourite movie on TV tonight. Are you going to watch it?

Going-to-Future: Aussagen (1)

① **Out of school**

School is over in ten minutes. Have a look at the students. What are their plans for the weekend? What are they going to do? Use the verbs from the box and write down sentences.

… is going to …
buy • go swimming • make • play (2x) • sleep • watch • write

---

1. _____
2. _____
3. _____
4. _____
5. _____
6. _____
7. _____
8. _____

Going-to-Future: Aussagen (2)

② **Class trip**

Your teacher is talking about the programme for your class trip. Write down what you are going to do.

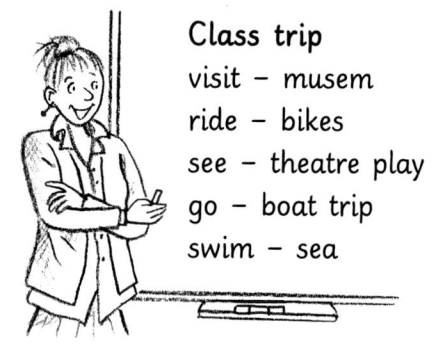

> Class trip
> visit – musem
> ride – bikes
> see – theatre play
> go – boat trip
> swim – sea

We are going to …

1. _____
2. _____
3. _____
4. _____
5. _____

③ **Complete the sentences. Use *going to* + the verbs from the box.**

| buy • do • give • ~~make~~ • take • visit • watch • wear |

1. It's my birthday tomorrow. I'm *going to make* a cake.

2. My sister cannot play with me. She _____ her homework.

3. It's raining, so I _____ the bus home.

4. I have some friends in London. I _____ them this weekend.

5. There's a party tonight. I _____ my new jeans.

6. There's nothing in the fridge. Mum _____ the food.

7. It's Olivia's birthday next week. We _____ her a present.

8. My favourite movie is on TV tonight. I _____ it.

Going-to-Future: Aussagen (1)

① Out of school

School is over in ten minutes. Have a look at the students. What are their plans for the weekend? What are they going to do? Use the words from below the pictures and write down sentences.

Schulschluss

In 10 Minuten ist die Schule aus. Schau dir die Schüler und Schülerinnen an. Was werden sie am Wochenende machen? Verwende die Begriffe unter den Bildern und bilde Sätze.

- buy tickets
- play football
- make a cake
- write a letter
- sleep in bed

Tim — Lisa — Bob

Josie — Harry

1. _____

2. _____

3. _____

4. _____

5. _____

Going-to-Future: Aussagen (2)

❷ Class trip

Your teacher is talking about the programme for your class trip.
Write down what you are going to do.

Klassenfahrt

Eure Lehrerin informiert euch über das Programm der Klassenfahrt.
Schreibe auf, was ihr unternehmen werdet.

Class trip
visit a musem
ride the bikes
see a theatre play
go on a boat trip
swim in the sea

We are going to …

1. _____ .
2. _____ .
3. _____ .
4. _____ .
5. _____ .

❸ Complete the sentences. Use *going to* + the verbs in brackets.

Vervollständige die Sätze. Verwende *going to* + die Verben in den Klammern.

It's my birthday tomorrow. I'm <u>*going to make*</u> a cake. (*make*)

My sister cannot play with me. She _____ her homework. (*do*)

It's raining, so I _____ the bus home. (*take*)

I have some friends in London. I _____ them this weekend. (*visit*)

There's a party tonight. I _____ my new jeans. (*wear*)

There's nothing in the fridge. Mum _____ the food. (*buy*)

It's Olivia's birthday next week. We _____ her a present. (*give*)

My favourite movie is on TV tonight. I _____ it. (*watch*)

Going-to-Future: Verneinung

① Write negative sentences.

1. I am going to go to Sam's party this weekend.

   I am not going to go to Sam's party this weekend.

2. She is going to celebrate her first birthday.

3. They are going to watch the match.

4. We are going to meet at the cinema.

5. He is going to invite her for dinner.

6. They are going to teach themselves French.

7. You are going to spend the Easter holidays with your grandparents.

8. I am going to have some drinks outside.

② Write 5 sentences about what you are not going to do the coming weekend.

1.
2.
3.
4.
5.

Going-to-Future: Verneinung

❶ Write negative sentences. Have a look at the example.
Schreibe verneinte Sätze. Achte auf das Beispiel.

> 💡 Don't forget how to use the negative form: am / is / are not going to …
> Denk daran, wie die verneinte Form gebildet wird: am / is / are going to …

1. I am going to go to Sam's party this weekend.

   I am not going to go to Sam's party this weekend.

2. She is going to celebrate her first birthday.

3. They are going to watch the match.

4. We are going to meet at the cinema.

5. He is going to invite her for dinner.

6. They are going to teach themselves French.

7. You are going to spend the Easter holidays with your grandparents.

❷ Write 4 sentences about what you are not going to do the coming weekend. You can take the ideas from the box.

Schreibe 4 Sätze darüber, was du am nächsten Wochenende nicht tun wirst. Du kannst auch Vorschläge aus der Box verwenden.

> walk the dog • do my homework • tidy up my room •
> visit my friends • play football • help in the garden • wash Dad's car

1. *I am not going to …*

2.

3.

4.

Going-to-Future: Fragen

① **Ask your friend what he/she is going to do for his/her next birthday party.**

1. _____

2. _____

3. _____

4. _____

5. _____

② **Fill in the *going to* form and complete the questions.**

1. Are you _____ ____ _____ (watch) the new Harry Potter movie?

2. ____ she _____ ____ _____ (make) a cake for her classmates?

3. _____ we _____ ____ _____ (buy) christmas presents?

4. _____ they _____ ____ _____ (help) you with the grocery?

Going-to-Future: Fragen

❶ **Ask your friend what he is going to do for his next birthday party. Have a look at the picture and the ideas from the box.**

Frage deinen Freund, was er für seine nächste Geburtstagsparty plant. Das Bild und die Begriffe in der Box helfen dir.

> Are you going to …?
> decorate the room • make sandwiches • buy drinks • write invitation cards •
> buy a new dress • have a DJ • dance with friends • buy flowers

1. _____

2. _____

3. _____

4. _____

❷ **Fill in the *going to* form and complete the questions. Have a look at the example.**

Setze die *going-to*-Form ein und vervollständige die Fragen. Achte auf das Beispiel.

Example: <u>Are</u> you <u>going</u> <u>to</u> <u>send</u> the invitation cards?

1. Are you _____ ___ _____ (watch) the new Harry Potter movie?

2. ____ she _____ ___ _____ (make) a cake for her classmates?

3. _____ we _____ ___ _____ (buy) christmas presents?

4. _____ they _____ ___ _____ (help) you with the grocery?

Will-Future

Grammar Box: Will-Future

Mit dem Will-Future drückst du aus, dass etwas irgendwann in der Zukunft passieren oder stattfinden wird. Du verwendest das Will-Future, um Vermutungen über die Zukunft auszudrücken. Häufig steht es auch nach Wendungen wie *I think* oder Ausdrücken wie *probably* („wahrscheinlich").

Bildung:

Du bildest das Will-Future mit *will* + Verb.

Verneinung:

Die verneinte Form von *will* ist *will not*. Hier kannst du auch die Kurzform *won't* verwenden.

Fragen:

Bei Fragen steht *will* am Anfang.

Will you have any children later? Wirst du später Kinder haben?

Will she become a doctor later? Wird sie später Ärztin werden?

Fragewörter + *will*:

When will she finish school?
Wann wird sie die Schule abschließen?

What will he do with all that money he won?
Was wird er mit dem ganzen Geld machen, das er gewonnen hat?

Will-Future: Aussagen

① **What will you have in ten years? Write down 5 sentences.**

1. _____
2. _____
3. _____
4. _____
5. _____

② **What will the students have in 10 years?**

Ben   Sarah   Olivia   Daniel   Rob   Lucy

1. *Ben will have a car.*
2. _____.
3. _____.
4. _____.
5. _____.
6. _____.

8 Will-Future: Aussagen

❶ What will you have in ten years? Write down 4 sentences.
Was wirst du in 10 Jahren haben? Schreibe 4 Sätze auf.

| big house • beautiful garden • fast car • be a millionaire • have a good job • have a family • have a dog • have a swimming pool |

In ten years …

1. I will have _____.

2. _____.

3. _____.

4. _____.

❷ What will the students have in 10 years? Write it down.
Was werden diese Personen in 10 Jahren haben? Schreibe auf.

Ben • Sarah • Olivia • Daniel • Rob • Lucy

1. *Ben will have a car.*

2. Sarah will have _____.

3. Olivia _____.

4. Daniel _____.

5. Rob _____.

6. Lucy _____.

© PERSEN Verlag   105

Will-Future: Verneinung (1)

① **Fill in *will* or *won't*.**

1. We can't go for a walk tomorrow because it _____ rain.

2. I _____ come to your party tomorrow because I'm ill.

3. I'm sure my friends _____ have a good time.

4. The students _____ fail this exam because it's very difficult.

5. I think they _____ win the match.

6. Probably I _____ have a fast car in 20 years.

② **Fortune teller**

Daniel wants to know about his life in ten years. Mrs Pink-Punk knows about his future. She tells him what he will or won't do in ten years. Write sentences and use *will* or *won't*.

- 👍 find a nice job
- 👎 become a millionaire
- 👍 have a dog
- 👎 have a cat
- 👍 spend holidays in Hollywood
- 👎 live in Hollywood
- 👍 have a girlfriend
- 👎 be married

1. *Daniel will find a nice job.*

2. He _____.

3. He _____.

4. He _____.

Will-Future: Verneinung (2)

5. *He won't become a millionaire.*

6. He _____ .

7. He _____ .

8. He _____ .

③ **Now you are Mrs Pink-Punk. Tell your friend about his/her life in ten years.**

These ideas might help you:
children • house • good friends • be married • job • rich • nice life • be happy • …

_____

_____

_____

_____

_____

Will-Future: Verneinung (1)

① Fill in *will* or *won't*. Have a look at the bold words.

Setze *will* oder *won't* ein. Achte auf die dick gedruckten Wörter.

We **can't go** for a walk tomorrow because it _____ rain.

I _____ come to your party tomorrow because **I'm ill**.

I'm sure my friends _____ have **a good time**.

The students _____ fail this exam because **it's very difficult** (*schwierig*).

I think they _____ **win** the match.

Probably I _____ have a fast car **in 20 years**.

② Fortune teller

Daniel wants to know about his life in ten years. Mrs Pink-Punk knows about his future. She tells him what he will or won't do in ten years. Write sentences and use *will* or *won't*.

Daniel möchte alles über seine Zukunft erfahren. Mrs Pink-Punk weiß es und erzählt ihm von seiner Zukunft. Bilde Sätze mit *will* und *won't*.

- find a nice job 👍
- become a millionaire 👎
- have a dog 👍
- have a cat 👎
- spend holidays in Hollywood 👍
- live in Hollywood 👎
- have a girfriend 👍
- be married 👎

1. *Daniel will find a nice job.*

2. He _____.

3. He _____.

4. He _____.

8 Will-Future: Verneinung (2)

5. *He won't become a millionaire.*

6. He _____ .

7. He _____ .

8. He _____ .

❸ Now you are Mrs Pink-Punk. Tell your friend about her life in ten years.

Stell dir vor, du bist Mrs Pink-Punk. Erzähle deiner Freundin über ihr Leben in zehn Jahren.

These ideas might help you:
children • house • good friends • be married • job • rich • nice life • be happy • …

In ten years you will …

_____

_____

_____

In ten years you won't …

_____

_____

_____

© PERSEN Verlag
109

Will-Future: Fragen

① **You are planning your holiday with a friend and you have a lot of questions. How will it be there?**

Write down the questions.

1. Wird das Wetter schön?

   _____?

2. Wird es dort regnen?

   _____?

3. Werden wir einen Regenmantel brauchen?

   _____?

4. Werden wir mit der U-Bahn fahren?

   _____?

5. Werden wir die Queen sehen?

   _____?

6. Werden die Leute dort nett sein?

   _____?

7. Wird es ein schöner Urlaub?

   _____?

8. Werden wir das englische Frühstück mögen?

   _____?

② **Write down three questions and ask your partner about his or her future life.**

1. _____?

2. _____?

3. _____?

8 Will-Future: Fragen

❶ You are planning your holiday trip to London with a friend and you have a lot of questions. How will it be there? Combine the right questions.

Du planst deinen Urlaub nach London mit einem Freund und ihr habt viele Fragen. Verbinde die Fragen richtig.

Wird das Wetter schön?	Will we need a raincoat?
Wird es dort regnen?	Will we see the queen?
Werden wir einen Regenmantel brauchen?	Will we like the English breakfast?
Werden wir mit der U-Bahn fahren?	Will the weather be nice?
Werden wir die Queen sehen?	Will it rain there?
Werden die Leute dort nett sein?	Will we take the tube?
Werden wir das englische Frühstück mögen?	Will the people be nice there?

❷ Choose three questions and ask your partner about his future life.

Wähle drei Fragen über die Zukunft aus und stelle sie deinem Partner.

> Will you have a family? • Will you become a football player? • Will you buy a house? • Will you have a dog? • Will you travel to London? • Will you go to university? • Will you become a teacher?

1. _____ ?

2. _____ ?

3. _____ ?

If-Satz Typ I

Grammar Box: If Clause Type I

Im If-Satz drückst du eine Bedingung aus, die sehr wahrscheinlich eintrifft.

Der If-Satz besteht immer aus einem Haupt- und einem Nebensatz. *If* bedeutet „falls, wenn".
Im Hauptsatz sagst du, was passiert, wenn diese Bedingung erfüllt wird.

Im If-Satz (Nebensatz) verwendest du das Simple Present, im Hauptsatz verwendest du das Will-Future.

Beispiele:

If you <u>learn</u> for the test, you <u>will get</u> a good mark.

Wenn du für den Test lernst, wirst du eine gute Note bekommen.

If the sun <u>shines</u>, we <u>will go</u> out for a walk.

Wenn die Sonne scheint, werden wir spazieren gehen.

If you <u>get up</u> early, you <u>won't come</u> late to school.

Wenn du früh aufstehst, wirst du nicht zu spät zur Schule kommen.

> Manchmal steht der Hauptsatz vorne und der Nebensatz hinten. In diesem Fall setzt du kein Komma zwischen Haupt- und Nebensatz!

I <u>will buy</u> a nice bag **if** I <u>get</u> this job.

Ich werde mir eine schöne Tasche kaufen, wenn ich diesen Job bekomme.

If-Satz Typ I: Übungen (1)

① **Holiday rules**

Find the right parts and match the sentences.

If you leave the house early,	you will be at the beach soon.
If you don't miss the train,	you will have a lot of fun.
If you are at the airport on time,	you will be at the airport on time.
If you catch the flight,	you won't get burned.
If you take a sun cream for the beach,	you won't miss the train.
If you meet new people there,	you will catch the flight.

If-Satz Typ I: Übungen (2)

② **What do the people say?**

Tim: _____ if you give me 5 €.

Mother: _____ if you don't take your jacket.

Lucy: _____ if you drop it.

Sarah: _____ if it doesn't rain.

Justin: _____ if it gets warmer.

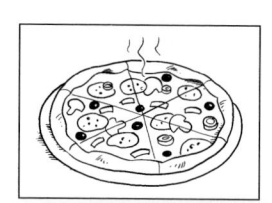

Sam: _____ if the fridge is empty.

If-Satz Typ I: Übungen (3)

3) If the weather is … Write down what you will do and what you won't do.

wet: stay at home – ~~go outside~~

If it's wet outside, I will stay at home. I won't go outside.

sunny: ~~listen to music~~ – play in the park

_____.

rainy: watch TV – ~~swim in the pool~~

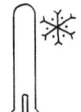

_____.

cold: ~~stay at home~~ – go skiing

_____.

windy: ~~go for a walk~~ – have a tea

_____.

4) If I don't tidy up my room, I won't see my friends.
Make if clauses.

a) Think about what will happen if you don't …

1. If I don't do my homework, _____.

2. If I don't learn for the test, _____.

3. If I don't tidy up my room, _____.

4. If I don't help my mum, _____.

b) Think about what will happen if you do …

1. If I wake up early, _____.

2. If I clean my bike, _____.

3. If I help my dad, _____.

4. If I go for a walk with the dog, _____.

If-Satz Typ I: Übungen (1)

❶ **Holiday rules**

Combine the pictures with the right sentences.

Urlaubsregeln

Ordne die Bilder den passenden Sätzen zu.

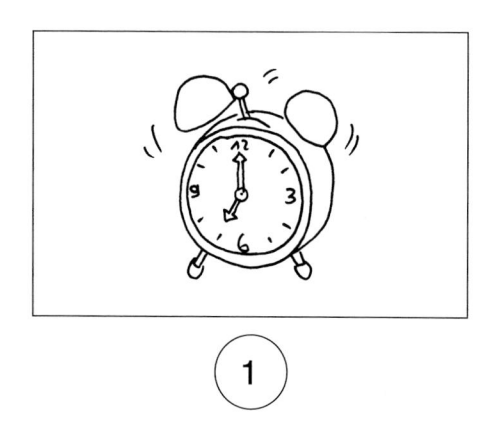

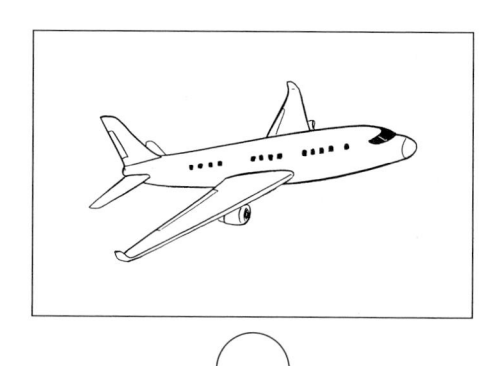

1. If you leave the house **early**, you won't miss the train.
2. If you don't miss the **train**, you will be at the airport on time.
3. If you are at the **airport** on time, you will catch the flight.
4. If you catch the **flight**, you will be at the beach soon.
5. If you take a sun cream for the **beach**, you won't get burned.
6. If you meet **new people** there, you will have a lot of fun.

If-Satz Typ I: Übungen (2)

❷ What do the people say? Combine the pictures with the right sentences.
Was sagen die Personen? Verbinde die Bilder mit den passenden Sätzen.

Mother: You'll get ill if you don't take your jacket.

Sarah: We'll have a picnic if it doesn't rain.

Sam: We'll order a pizza if the fridge is empty.

Justin: I'll buy an ice cream, if it gets warmer.

Tim: I'll do the shopping if you give me 5 €.

Lucy: The mirror will break if you drop it.

9 If-Satz Typ I: Übungen (3)

❸ If the weather is nice … Write down what you will do.

Wenn das Wetter gut ist … Schreibe auf, was du tun wirst.

wet: stay at home – ~~go outside~~

If it's wet outside, *I will stay at home*. I won't *go outside*.

sunny: ~~listen to music~~ – play in the park

If it's sunny, _____ . I won't _____ .

rainy: watch TV – ~~swim in the pool~~

If it's rainy, _____ . I won't _____ .

cold: ~~stay at home~~ – go skiing

If it's cold, _____ . I won't _____ .

windy: ~~go for a walk~~ – have a tea

If it's windy, _____ . I won't _____ .

❹ If I don't tidy up my room, I won't see my friends. Fill in the blanks.

Wenn ich mein Zimmer nicht aufräume, werde ich meine Freunde nicht treffen. Fülle die Lücken.

> you won't ride your bike in the park • I won't see my friends • she will be angry • my friends won't come • I will get a bad mark • my teacher will be angry

1. If I don't do my homework, _____ .

2. If I don't learn for the test, _____ .

3. If I don't tidy up my room, _____ .

4. If I don't help my mum, _____ .

5. If I don't go outside, _____ .

6. If I don't repair your bike, _____ .

Abbildungsverzeichnis

Mehrfach verwendete Illustrationen sind nur bei Erstabbildung genannt.

Cover und Kapitelpiktogramme: Stefan Lucas;

S. 7:	Fuchs: Kristina Klotz, Glühbirne: Katharina Reichert-Scarborough;
S. 8:	Hausaufgaben: Julia Flasche;
S. 12:	Bananen, Pizza, Klassenzimmer, Fahrrad, Küche, Fußball: Katharina Reichert-Scarborough, Äpfel: Tina Pohl, Spaghetti, Tennis: Julia Flasche, Schaukel: Barbara Gerth, Katze, Hund: Corina Beurenmeister;
S. 15:	Wecker: Corina Beurenmeister;
S. 18:	Kino: Steffen Jähde, T-Shirts kaufen: Barbara Gerth, Fahrrad-Reparatur: Corina Beurenmeister, Fußball spielende Kinder: Katharina Reichert-Scarborough, Staubsaugen: Julia Flasche;
S. 19:	Wortschlange: Barbara Gerth;
S. 24:	Computerspiel: Mele Brink, tanzende Großeltern: Bettina Weyland, Hausaufgaben: Katharina Reichert-Scarborough, Gitarre spielendes Mädchen: Barbara Gerth;
S. 25:	Eis: Katharina Reichert-Scarborough;
S. 29:	Mädchen macht Hausaufgaben, Park: Barbara Gerth, Einladung: Nataly Meenen, Hotel: Katharina Reichert-Scarborough, Küche putzen: Mele Brink;
S. 30:	Postkarte: Barbara Gerth, Sandwich: Corina Beurenmeister;
S. 35:	Junge mit Hund: Julia Flasche;
S. 36:	Fernsehen: Elisabeth Lottermoser;
S. 42:	Kaffee: Corina Beurenmeister;
S. 43:	Zoo: Barbara Gerth;
S. 48:	Lupe: Katharina Reichert-Scarborough;
S. 50:	Sinne: Ute Ohlms;
S. 52:	Familie, Pferd: Corina Beurenmeister, Maus: Anke Fröhlich, Schmetterling: Steffi Aufmuth;
S. 53:	Thermometer, Autos: Barbara Gerth;
S. 54:	Torte: Barbara Gerth;
S. 57:	Riese, Zwerg, Hosen, Sonne, Regen: Barbara Gerth, Mäuse, Daumen hoch, Smiley schlecht: Katharina Reichert-Scarborough;
S. 65:	Lachender Junge: Charlotte Wagner;
S. 66:	Stift: Barbara Gerth;
S. 70:	Mädchen mit Buch: Julia Flasche, Bücherstapel: Corina Beurenmeister, Stift: Katharina Reichert-Scarborough, Taschen: Barbara Gerth;
S. 74:	Kühlschrank: Corina Beurenmeister, Notiz (ohne Beschriftung): Kristina Klotz;
S. 75:	Schultasche mit Inhalt: Heike Heimrich, Einkaufen: Carla Miller;
S. 79:	Geld: Carla Miller, Stau: Corina Beurenmeister, Party: Barbara Gerth, Museum: Kristina Klotz;

Abbildungsverzeichnis

S. 85: Ordnung/Unordnung: Sabine Voigt, Koffer, schmutziges Geschirr: Julia Flasche, Geschirr spülen: Rebecca Meyer, Postkarte, schmutziger Junge, duschender Junge: Corina Beurenmeister, leerer Kühlschrank: Kristina Klotz;

S. 86: Hefte vergessen, Bus verpasst, Sieger, kaputte Tasse: Corina Beurenmeister, Wandergruppe: Stefan Lucas;

S. 90: Geburtstagsparty: Barbara Gerth;

S. 91: Geld: Elisabeth Lottermoser;

S. 92: Taucher: Bettina Weller;

S. 93: Frau mit Sprechblase (ohne Beschriftung): Petra Lefin;

S. 95: Klasse, Tickets, schreiben, Schlagzeug: Corina Beurenmeister, Kuchen, Bett: Julia Flasche, Fernseher: Katharina Reichert-Scarborough, Schwimmutensilien: Mele Brink;

S. 96: Lehrerin vor Tafel (ohne Beschriftung): Katharina Reichert-Scarborough;

S. 101: Gartenparty: Katharina Reichert-Scarborough;

S. 104: Hunde: Corina Beurenmeister, Haus: Tina Pohl, Farm: Barbara Gerth, Schüler: Julia Flasche;

S. 106: Wahrsagerin: Steffen Jähde, Daumen: Julia Flasche;

S. 107: Glaskugel: Christina Piper;

S. 110: Freunde: Katharina Reichert-Scarborough, Flagge: Kristina Klotz;

S. 113: Strand, Flugzeug, Beachball: Steffen Jähde, Zug: Barbara Gerth, Flughafen: Mele Brink;

S. 114: Krankes Kind: Corina Beurenmeister, Spiegel, Picknick: Julia Flasche, Eis: Barbara Gerth;

S. 115: Thermometer, Wind, Pfütze: Corina Beurenmeister, Sonne: Barbara Gerth